What else do you do?

Picture the scene. I am at a party in NW1 (or it could be
Islington) and I am hemmed in a corner between a tall, fair man
who is something in advertising and a tall, dark girl.

I mutter something very clever, like, 'Hello'.

The tall girl looks down for a brief moment. 'Hello. And what
do you do?'

'I am a cartoonist,' I say.

'Oh, what FUN,' she says.

'Not really,' I say.

'Fascinating,' the man in advertising says. 'What else do you
do?'

I've been looking at where his ideas come from and it's really messy ... down there...
RING! RING!

Mel Calman

What else do you do?

Some sketches from a cartoonist's life

A Methuen Paperback

by the same author

This Pestered Isle (*Times Newspapers Ltd*)
Couples (*The Workshop*)
But it's my turn to leave you . . . (*Methuen*)
How about a little quarrel before bed? (*Methuen*)
Help! (*Methuen*)
Calman Revisited (*Methuen*)
The Big Novel (*Methuen*)
My God (*Methuen*)
It's only you that's incompatible (*Methuen*)

First published 1986
This paperback edition first published 1987
by Methuen London Ltd, 11 New Fetter Lane, London EC4P 4EE

Copyright © Mel Calman 1986
Designed by Philip Thompson

Printed in Great Britain by
Redwood Burn Ltd, Trowbridge, Wiltshire

British Library Cataloguing in Publication Data

Calman, Mel
    What else do you do? : some sketches
    from a cartoonist's life.
    1. Calman, Mel   2. Cartoonists—Great
    Britain—Biography
    I. Title
    741'.092'4   NC1479.C33
    ISBN 0–413–17310–0

The chapters on National Service were first published in *All Bull* (edited by B. S. Johnson), published by Allison and Busby, 1973.

The pages from various newspapers and periodicals are reproduced with due acknowledgement to their source, and the letters on p. 103 by the kind permission of Captain Nunn of the Royal Marines.

Contents

To Debby – who laughed when I sat down to write

Bet she stopped
as soon as she
read it...

PUNCH
10 BOUVERIE STREET
LONDON
E.C.4

TELEGRAMS:
CHARIVARI, FLEET, LONDON

TELEPHONE:
FLEET STREET 9161 (6 LINES)

18th. September,
1956.

Melville S. Calman, Esq.,
64, Linthorpe Road,
London. N.16.

Dear Calman,

　　　　I rather doubt if "cartooning" (as it
is generally called) is really your line.
Neither drawings or ideas measure up to the
standard required here, I'm afraid.

　　　　"City/Country" is a closed shop;
we have two artists quite good at it and
only one can we use.

　　　　Many regrets.

Russell Brockbank

To whom it may concern

Picture the scene. I am at a party in NW1 (or it could be Islington) and I am hemmed in a corner between a tall, fair man who is something in advertising and a tall, dark girl who works for the BBC (or possibly Channel 4). They are deeply in love with each other and are talking avidly to each other's egos.

I mutter something very clever, like, 'Hello'.

The tall girl looks down for a brief moment. 'Hello. And what do you do?'

'I am a cartoonist,' I say.

'Oh, what FUN,' she says.

'Not really,' I say.

'Fascinating,' the man in advertising says. 'What else do you do?'

I make my excuses and leave, as they say in the papers.

It is my least favourite question and the one most often asked. (Another delightful question is, 'Who writes your captions?')

This book is an attempt to explain what I do and why I do it. And a little bit extra on how I came to be doing it in the first place.

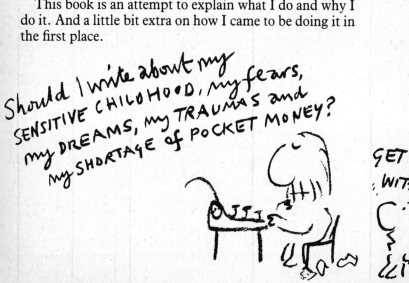

Should I write about my SENSITIVE CHILDHOOD, my fears, my DREAMS, my TRAUMAS and my SHORTAGE of POCKET MONEY?

GET ON WITH IT!

1 . The road to Cambridge University is paved with pull doors

I cannot remember ever deciding to become a cartoonist: I seem to have slid into it in the way that some criminals say they slid onto the wrong side of the law. One minute I was a fresh-faced youth imagining that I could be a film director – or, at least a journalist, like my older brother – and the next minute, here I am: wrinkled, middle-aged and cartooning all over the place. Did God plan it? Did I? Was it all accident or Fate?

I was born in Stamford Hill, in North London. Stamford Hill was a sort of staging post for Jews on their way from Whitechapel to Hampstead and Golders Green. Most of our neighbours were small business men, taxi drivers and musicians. Harry Roy, who had his own band, had lived nearly opposite our house, before he made the big time and moved 'up West'.

It was a lovely place for a child; there was a pond for sailing small boats, a park for running about in, two cinemas, an ABC teashop, a public library, a Grodzinski bakery in Dunsmure Road which made the best jam doughnuts in the world, and a dry cleaner's with a new-fangled machine in the window, where you could watch (free of charge) clothes spinning round and round.

When war broke out we survived the Blitz by going every night to a shelter at the top of our road, carrying blankets, thermos flasks and sandwiches. Every morning we emerged like dusty moles into the light and I would pick up pieces of still-hot shrapnel to take home to my collection. My older brother, Monte, joined the Army and was posted to Cambridge. The Blitz became more alarming and my mother decided that we should join him in Cambridge.

As a schoolboy in Cambridge I devoured films and saw as many as I could, often going three times a week. In those days cinemas showed a different programme on Sundays, which meant that an addict could get extra doses of the hard stuff if he needed it badly.

I loved all films: everything from glossy musicals with Esther Williams grinning to sleazy thrillers with James Cagney dying. My older sister, Lydia, shared this passion and we often went together. Because of the war and the subsequent shortage of journalists, she had managed to persuade the *Cambridge Daily News* to use her as a film reviewer. If she couldn't find a suitable boyfriend, she took me along as her companion. Each reviewer was allocated a different cinema and hers was the Rex. This meant that she had to see everything the Rex showed – regardless of merit. This was an educational experience. It taught me to enjoy the films that now get shown late at night on Channel Four.

I even learnt something of the techniques of journalism by helping her struggle through her reviews. ('Also featured was that old favourite, Eugene Palette, in the minor role of the irascible father, whilst the direction was in the firm hands of . . .') We left no cliché unturned in our desperate search for a writing style. During this period I also entertained strong fantasies of becoming a cinema manager, standing there in my dinner jacket, seeing all the films for nothing.

The reality was an intense, rather anxious scholarship boy at the Perse School, struggling with Latin grammar and the intrigues of Cromwell. The Perse was full of clever youths, all intent on making brilliant careers. The school expected everyone to go to Cambridge University – anything less was heresy.

I was in the same sixth form as Peter Hall, and he set the pace for everyone else. The English master, Mr Wollman, would listen carefully to all Peter's opinions on the text (we were studying *Hamlet* that year), nod approval, then move down the glittering rows, gathering nuggets of considered brilliance and insight. By the time he got to me, I felt that there was nothing left to say.

I was very keen on the theatre and joined the Perse Players, an amateur group inside the school which put on a full-scale production of a Shakespeare play every year. I worked my way up from a member of the rabble in *Julius Caesar*, muttering 'rhubarb, rhubarb,' to the dizzy heights of Third Player in *Hamlet*. Peter Hall, I need hardly say, was Hamlet. Still, my part was crucial. I got to pour the poison in the King's ear – and the whole plot does

To Peter Hall or Not to Peter Hall..

rather hang on this murder.

I suffered terrible stage-fright and dreamt that I had forgotten my lines. On the night, I delivered my single speech without a mistake and then went out into the night, aglow with self-satisfaction.

At the bus stop I met Mr Wollman, who was there.

'Good evening, Calman,' he boomed. He had a very low, deep voice which made him sound more pompous than he was. 'How did you enjoy the play?'

'Very much, sir,' I said proudly. 'I was in it.'

'Really?' he said. 'I didn't notice.'

In spite of a certain lack of official encouragement, I did try to enter Cambridge University. I got an interview with the Senior Tutor at St Catharine's College and arrived on the day, nice and early. I knocked on the door and there was silence. 'I must be too early,' I thought. So I waited until two o'clock – at the time of my interview – and knocked again. Silence. I saw no one on the staircase to ask for advice, so waited patiently and occasionally tried the handle of the door. I would still be there today, waiting for the Senior Tutor to arrive, if I hadn't inadvertently pulled the door towards me, in a rage of frustration. The door opened and I realised that I had been trying to *push* open a *pull*-kind of door. The pull door was a soundproof door, hiding another door to his inner sanctum – which explained why he had not heard my frantic knocking.

I was now fifteen minutes late. The Senior Tutor was sitting at his desk, in front of a cosy fire, working at a pile of papers. I apologised and explained why I was late. I did not have the sense to invent a sick grandmother; I simply told the truth. He looked at me and smiled. It was not a reassuring smile.

'Well,' he said, 'you seem to have failed the first intelligence test.'

So at eighteen I found myself looking for a career that would have me. I wanted to do something interesting and creative before National Service grabbed me. My Higher Certificate results were slightly below poor – apart from English. My father died, and the family decided I should return to London.

My first plan was to become a journalist. I wanted to work in Fleet Street, which seemed glamorous to me. I went (with my sister for moral support) to the Regent

ART | LIFE

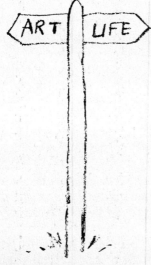

Try both...

Street Poly, which then had a successful course in journalism. The course was full, so we crossed the corridor to try the Art School. I had always enjoyed drawing in my spare time, even though I showed little sign of talent. The art course was also full, but the secretary suggested I try the Borough Polytechnic Art School. This was August and most art schools had already chosen their students, so there was little time to pick and choose.

I did not even know where the Borough was; North Londoners try to avoid crossing the river Thames – one doesn't know where it's been. We hot-footed it over to the Borough Poly and saw the Principal.

He was a short, grey-haired, kindly man who had once been in charge of a catering school before he had landed up on the shores of Art. (Someone told me that he was an expert in cake decoration.) I didn't show him my folder of work, for the simple reason that I didn't have one. All I had was a desperate desire to get in out of the cold.

Fortunately for me, although I did not know it at the time, the Borough Art School was short of its quota of students. This was in the long-distant past when the adult education system was actually looking for people to educate.

Perhaps my desperation made me sound more talented than I was, for I was accepted and we discussed the courses available.

'What kinds of art are there?' I asked, diffidently.

'There's Fine Art, Illustration and Commercial Art.'

I paused, totally at a loss.

'Well, you said you were interested in writing as well as drawing, so why not try Illustration?' he said.

So I chose Illustration and took the first fatal step on the road to cartooning.

We hurried back home to tell the rest of the family the good news. My mother was delighted; my aunt was cautious (but she was cautious about everything and could take an hour to decide if she should have another cup of tea); and my brother said, 'How can you go to art school when you can't draw?'

2. Across the river and into the HBs

In September I crossed the river to the Borough for my first day at the art school. I travelled all the way with this lump in my stomach. I felt as sick and anxious as I did on my first day at primary school when my mother left me in the playground and I felt I would never see her again.

When I came out of the tube station I felt worse: the area seemed very alien, windswept and sad. I looked at the bombsites (this was 1949 and most of London had not yet been redeveloped). I looked at the little knots of crumpled old ladies standing on street corners gossiping to each other and I ached to get back to cosy Stamford Hill.

The Poly was large and characterless and everyone seemed to know where they were going – except me. What was I doing here? I knew nothing about proper drawing. All I knew about art was that I liked it. Was an appreciation of Van Gogh's *Sunflowers*, as last seen in Heffer's window in Cambridge, really an adequate preparation for studying art? What if I had to draw a nude woman on my first day? I dismissed such an absurd idea. One obviously began with plants and stones – like we did at school, then linocuts and then, next year, perhaps, nude women.

To calm my nerves I went to find the little shop that sold art materials and bought a drawing board, two pencils, a soft rubber, four drawing pins and two sheets of cartridge paper. I was now ready for action.

I then found the studio listed on the timetable and entered. The first thing I noticed was the wonderful smell of oil and turpentine. I had never smelt this potent combination before and I fell in love with it. The room was large and scruffy, with easels and 'donkeys' (an easel that you sit at, with legs astride) arranged in a semi-circle around a low platform. All the students seemed to be older than me – they had obviously done their National Service or even served in the war. One student standing nearby, smoking a pipe and wearing a velvet cord jacket, looked exactly like an illustration for Du Maurier's *Trilby*.

He had the studied look of casual nonchalance that I told myself hid enormous insecurity.

'Where can I sit?' I asked him in a whisper, as if I was interrupting a church service.

He stopped mixing the colours on his palette and gestured expansively round the room. 'Anywhere. It's Liberty Hall.' I took the first empty 'donkey' I could see and propped up my board against it. A young girl sitting on the platform, huddled up against a small electric fire, suddenly stood up, took off her thin dressing gown and there she was – the first *naked* woman I had ever seen in my life (apart from glimpses of my mother in her corset).

I now had two major problems. One, I hadn't the faintest idea of how to start drawing the female figure. Two, I was too shy to look at this nude woman. I could almost hear my mother's voice saying, 'Melville, what are you doing? Stop that at once.'

I slowly pinned one sheet of paper on to the board. Then, to give me time to think, I fiddled with the 'donkey' and adjusted it. And then, when I could avoid it no longer I started to draw. I kept peeping out at the model from behind the drawing board and retreating back to the drawing. It was more like drawing from memory than life drawing.

After half an hour, I had drawn this strange tiny figure cramped up into a corner of what seemed an enormous sheet of white paper. It looked more like a dead insect than a live woman.

The art teacher appeared and sat down beside me. Then, quietly, like a doctor talking to a patient with an incurable disease, he began to explain what was wrong with the drawing. He drew quickly and fluently alongside my deformed scribble. He talked of cones and cylinders; he talked of muscles and *gluteus maximuses*; he talked of proportion and symmetry; and he talked of balance and how the model was standing on one foot more than the other. I began to sweat with panic. All I had noticed was the nudeness and nothing else.

Thank God the coffee break arrived and saved me from further embarrassment. I went off with everyone else to the canteen to recover my nerve. I had no idea that drawing could be such hard work. I returned refreshed and ready for further punishment.

There was a small group gathered round my easel and they appeared to be laughing at something.

'What's wrong?' I asked nervously.

'Nothing,' said one, trying hard to stifle his giggles. 'Nothing . . . it's . . . er . . . er your drawing . . . it's full of character.'

After that, I never left the room without carefully covering my drawing so that it could not be seen by anyone else.

3. Looking for the green highlights

I slowly and painfully learned the basic grammar of drawing so that I could get through the classes without everyone else falling about in giggles.

The art school contained a curious mix of students. A large group were Polish exiles who clung together and only spoke Polish or extremely broken English; entering the canteen on some days was like entering Eastern Europe – I half expected to be asked for my passport. They were older than the other students and one man had even been in the Polish Resistance.

Another group were tough-talking Cockneys, wanting to be commercial artists. These students used the airbrush and bad language with equal expertise.

Yet another group came at nights to worship at the feet (or palette) of David Bomberg, who taught painting; all his students considered themselves more like disciples than mere students. I was too young to understand their Expressionist aims and every time I brushed against a paint-spattered chair or easel I wondered how they could afford to waste so much paint.

My principal teacher was an old pro, who loved to demonstrate his slick techniques with pencil and brush. He chain-smoked and his clothes were always covered in ash, like grey dandruff. He would draw all over my hesitant scratches, mixing his smudged highlights with the cigarette ash that dropped from his ever-present fags. I used to watch, fascinated, as the ash grew on the end of his cigarette, and wonder if he would take any evasive action to stop it falling on to my drawing. He never did, and when the ash fell, he would casually brush it into the paper, with a nonchalant laugh.

We did not exactly like each other: he sensed that I secretly despised his slick skills, even though I tried again and again to copy them. It was hopeless. I have never been able to learn techniques; if I had, who knows what heights of dexterity I might have reached by now?

He also tried to teach me anatomy and perspective. (Composition was taught by someone else.) The training was extremely academic, even for the early Fifties.

We had to learn arbitrary rules about picture-making. We were not allowed, for example, to cut off the human figure, even in the foreground. Everyone had to be drawn full-length; it was as if Degas and Lautrec had never lived.

There was much talk of 'pyramids in composition' and 'leading the eye round' (which can be very uncomfortable) and 'into the picture'. I was always being urged to look for the green shadows under the chin of the model. I could never see those green shadows and had to pretend to – just to be polite.

We drew from the plaster cast as well as from the live model. I remember long, heavy afternoons of drudgery, staring at casts of Voltaire and Michelangelo's *David*. It was enough to put you off Art for life.

One afternoon a week we had a still-life class, where we attempted to paint (in water-colour) artfully arranged groups of vases, flowers and sometimes, as a visual treat, two dead herrings. These classes were another opportunity for Mr Smudged Highlights, the smoker, to come and demonstrate his skills. I expect he meant well, but his facility only gave me stage-fright.

I enjoyed stretching the paper on the drawing board, but the thought of spoiling all that virgin white space paralysed my hand.

'Be bold,' he would urge me. 'Don't be afraid of it. Look for the green highlights under the mauve cloth.' He was keen on mauve backcloths for the groups and I have never really liked mauve since then. Still, I learned how to stretch paper – always useful.

The perspective classes were even greater agony. I tried to draw all my lines nicely up to the V.P. (Vanishing Point) but somewhere, somehow, they contrived to wander off-course. I have enormous respect for the Renaissance, but I have never properly understood how perspective works, nor even why it matters. I am a natural Primitive, I suppose. But you had to pass an examination in perspective (as well as the other subjects) to get your Intermediate certificate – so I sweated on.

We also had to acquire a nodding relationship with clay-modelling, wood-engraving and life-drawing. I finally managed to look at the naked ladies without sweating with embarrassment. They were often rather sad women, much given to staring unhappily into space, while they tried to cover their appendectomy scars with their blue-from-cold hands.

One actually burst into tears and ran off, out of the studio, never to return. I always wondered if it was because she had seen my drawing of her.

I yearned, and still do, to be able to do justice to the female body. I wanted to possess the skill of Degas to recreate that beauty on the white sheet of paper. I did try. I learned to look; really *look*, not simply stare. I learned to understand something of the structure of the human figure. I tried to convert all that looking into pencil marks. But in the end, art school taught me to recognise my limitations, and I think that was the most useful thing I learned.

Once I realised that I had no natural facility, I had to develop the rest of my skills, and that led me to living by my wits. I had to think about graphic solutions when I could not rely on drawing tricks to rescue me. I am certain that working within strict limits encourages people to think. When I teach art students now, I try to make them use their minds before they pick up a pencil. Sometimes students imagine that a picture will appear, by magic, if they tickle the paper often enough.

4. Absolute Fifties

1951 was an exciting year: the Festival of Britain opened
on the South Bank and I changed art schools. Despite my
pessimistic feelings about my lack of facility I had passed
my Intermediate exams in Arts and Crafts and used this
minor triumph to get into St Martin's School in Soho.

Soho seemed very exciting and cosmopolitan after the
Borough. There were interesting food shops, little cafés
full of French and Italians talking loudly to each other and
prostitutes on street corners, whispering 'Hello, *chéri*' in
phoney-sounding French accents. It was like being abroad
– not that I had yet been abroad.

I rather liked being accosted by women every time I
went out for a coffee to Patisserie Valerie in Old Compton
Street. In Stamford Hill, one was only accosted by rabbis
looking for the way to Manor House tube station.

Valerie's became the centre of my life at St Martin's. We
went there for morning coffee (unless we went to the café
known as 'The French' – where the coffee tasted only of
chicory), for afternoon tea and for spare bits in between. It
was our second common room and we would reluctantly
leave to return to our life classes and the goose-pimpled
models.

I still go to Valerie's and savour the atmosphere. There
are differences: a pot of tea costs 60p (12*s.*) instead of 5p
(1*s.*). It is now Italian instead of Belgian: the *patronne* used
to sit beside the splendid marble counter, wearing her
cloche hat and holding court with all her cronies. And, of
course, people managed to drink their coffee without
having their Filofaxes on the table beside them.

I wish I could tell you vibrant tales of life in the Fifties;
of jiving till dawn; of drinking with Dylan Thomas in
Fitzrovia; of helping Colin MacInnes to write *Absolute
Beginners*.

The truth is a little paler than that. I jived at parties,
but, apart from one exciting night when I missed the last
bus and slept all night on two chairs, I was always home

On a clear day
you can see
Jeffrey Bernard...

before dawn. I once spoke to Colin MacInnes at a party, but cannot remember a word of what we said to each other. Probably something literary, like, 'Where do they keep the booze here?'

I went to the theatre a great deal: I saw Ralph Richardson and Michael Redgrave at the New Theatre for 2s. 6d. (with sixpence extra for the gallery queue stool).

I joined the British Film Institute, which held weekly screenings of World Cinema Classics at the Institut Français, and then later at its brand-new cinema on the South Bank. I hoped to meet some female soul-mate at these screenings but they always seemed to be full of pale, bearded, young men who knew the name of the assistant sound recordist on *The Battleship Potemkin*.

I saw all those French films, like *Les Enfants du Paradis* at the Academy Cinema, that make one fall in love with France and being unhappy. I saw Jean Gabin dying in his attic (*Le Jour se Lève*); Jean Marais dying in his forest (*La Belle et La Bête*); Louis Jouvet dying in his hotel room (*Hotel du Nord*). I began to think that the only way to live was to die. Preferably in French with English sub-titles.

Ah- Les Subtitles du Paradis..

I became that odd creature – an art student. I wanted to be a romantic figure bursting with sex and passion, yet I still lived at home with my family in Stamford Hill. That is why jazz became so potent for me. Jazz was a world where a momma was a big black lady full of gin and good times, and not a woman asking if you were wearing a vest.

I remember reading Rudi Blesh's book about jazz, *Shining Trumpets*, and being so fired with enthusiasm for this magic music (full of protest, love and sex) that I rushed out and bought a second-hand Jelly Roll Morton record, even though I still did not have a record player.

Every time I entered the common room at St Martin's, I was blasted by the sound of Earl Bostic playing 'Flamingo' on the battered gramophone. (For those people who do not know what Earl Bostic sounded like – he played a very hard, driving alto sax, as if he wanted to singe your eardrums.)

One friend, Marian, who had more sophisticated tastes in music than I did – she only liked modern jazz – introduced me to all the jazz clubs. We would go and stand in extreme discomfort to listen to all this wonderful noise.

Ronnie Scott's was then in Gerrard Street; a narrow

tunnel of a place with a few broken chairs and a small quantity of very un-fresh air. It was a mistake to try and use this air, since it smelled of unwashed bodies and dope.

I went alone to the homes of traditional jazz: the 100 Club in Oxford Street, and the Ken Colyer Club in Great Windmill Street, where Chris Barber played. I did some jiving, but never managed the art of keeping a girl interested enough to see me another night.

I don't quite know what was wrong with my sexual techniques, but they were primitive. I was shy and would consider the right verbal approach for so long that the prospective victim would have been spotted and bagged by another man before I could say 'hello'.

I did have a girlfriend for a while – a Jewish girl who went out with me to films and concerts. She also allowed a limited amount of fumbling in doorways and on special occasions in her family sitting room, if her mother was out. She eventually dropped me because she wanted to save herself for a suitable husband, and she considered an art student a bad financial risk. She was right, of course.

While I was at St Martin's I started a magazine. I felt that I needed one place which would accept my drawings. I persuaded the Students Union that we needed a magazine to foster communications between the students and provide a platform for their views. 'Who will edit this magazine?' someone asked. There was a short silence and I quickly volunteered before anyone else could step in. I called it, *Fourth Floor* because the title sounded plain and un-arty and because the art school was on the fourth floor.

I wrote to several famous artists for contributions and some said, 'No' but John Minton, L. S. Lowry and Carel Weight all wrote short pieces. I wrote the rest of the first issue myself – not out of vanity but out of desperation, when no other students delivered anything. I wrote several humorous parodies and pieces – mostly in a sub-S. J. Perelman manner.

I knew nothing about printing or typography and so had to find an accomplice to help me. Someone mentioned that Len Deighton (who was studying Graphics) knew something about magazines, as he had actually produced one of his own.

I went to see him. He lived in one room above a tailor's in Soho, totally surrounded by clutter, newspapers, magazines, photographs and a pressure cooker. I think he cooked everything (apart from toast) in that cooker. I thought that the room was wonderfully Bohemian – not a Jewish mother in sight. I ached with envy at the splendid squalor of it all.

Len seemed able to talk, eat, wave his arms and laugh at the same time and made me feel that anything was possible. He agreed to help me and immediately reached for the telephone to persuade a typographer friend to come round and help us.

In fact, the friend did all the typography whilst Len and I argued about the titles of the various pieces. Len offered to draw the first cover himself. It showed two art students – the girl wearing the art school uniform of the Fifties, a wasp belt and a flared skirt, walking towards a sign: 'Soho-Foreign Spoke here'. I said that it was too parochial if we wanted to sell the magazine outside the art school. Len disagreed with me, but said, 'Don't worry. I'll do something else.'

A day before we had to take everything to the printers, Len showed me the same cover drawing, now made up into process blocks. He had used up my remaining funds on this cover so that I had no choice but to use it. It was Len's cover or a blank page.

I was furious. 'I'm the editor,' I thought. 'How can he do this?'

'He's done it,' I replied to myself.

Len taught me that there is more to being an editor than knowing about English grammar. He also made me think that he might go on to be successful at something or other.

I was very pleased with the final result – especially the way my name looked against the title of 'editor'. We sold nearly all our printed copies (it cost 6d. a copy) and I dutifully sent off copies to the outside contributors, as I felt a proper magazine would do. I was slightly less pleased with myself when I got a friendly letter from John Minton, pointing out that I needed a contents page next time.

Apart from my education in cinematic suffering and magazine editing I also tried to study Art. I carried a sketchbook everywhere. I drew people and rubbed them out and redrew them – and they still didn't look right.

We went out sketching with our large boards, mostly drawing street markets. I enjoyed the outings away from the art school, apart from the young kids who stood behind me telling me what was wrong with my drawing – 'Look mister, you put in three windows and there are five'. Pick up a pencil and everyone is an art critic.

The set book of that year's exams (the National Diploma in Design) was H. G. Wells's *Invisible Man* and I struggled to make my drawings reflect the flavour of the book, which I loved. I caught the humour of the book – but the frightening parts became unconsciously funny. I drew the Invisible Man wearing his bandages, hoping that he would look alarming – but he only looked cuddly.

I had to design a symbol for UNO for some project and when my tutor saw my version (two hands holding a perfectly serious globe) he smiled and laughed. I think that my pencil was trying to tell me something, but I was not yet ready to listen.

John Ward, who taught drawing at St Martin's, tried in vain to persuade me to draw more precisely. He did communicate, however, a great appreciation of what drawing meant to him. I watched him pick up a fine pen and draw the details of a window in the National Gallery, and envied that degree of concentration in hand and eye.

I am not certain that I learnt anything useful about being funny at art school – but I did learn something about the ways that marks on paper can suggest reality. And reality was fast approaching in the shape of large sergeants with loud voices. In those days every healthy male had to do two years' National Service.

5. National disservice

The first mistake I made was taking my moustache into the Army with me. I had had a beard at art school, and kept the moustache as a souvenir of the beard. But amongst the fresh chins of the eighteen-year-olds, my moustache could be seen at a hundred paces and marked me as if I had been painted red. Every time I footfaulted myself at drill, I was noticed immediately and the drill sergeant bellowed out:

'Who's that horrible man with a 'tache . . . stand still when I'm talking to you!'

After four years at an art school I suddenly found myself in an establishment that was half adult boarding school, half lunatic asylum. The masters were the officers, the prefects were the NCOs and the rules were rampant and completely arbitrary.

You had to polish the barrack-room bucket, knowing it would get dirty and have to be polished again the next day. You had to remove all the lettering from the lid of your boot-polish tin and make it mirror-shine for inspections. (So you bought two tins: one for use, one for show.) You had to fold your sheets and blankets every morning in certain ritualised ways. You had to greet other men with special salutes that involved twisting your neck, your wrist, your dignity. You had to move by numbers: turn, two, three, breathe in, pause, two, three, breathe out. You had to stop thinking 'why' and do it. You had to unlearn being an individual and become a number and put that number on all your clothes and on your soul, if told to. An Army requires instant obedience, because death requires instant obedience. You cannot say to the Angel of Death, 'I'm not coming with you. Why should I?'

After basic training, we heard rumours that you were allowed to regain some of your personality. Even wear shoes sometimes instead of boots. Find some quiet niche where you could hibernate for the rest of the two years.

I had put my name down for the niche labelled 'Education Corps'. I had an art teacher's certificate and a smear of education and it seemed a waste not to use any of it. But I had also learned that Education Corps sergeants (and everyone in the Corps was a sergeant or higher) had a room of their own. I did not like barrack-room life. The last thing a private got was any privacy.

There were others in the barracks going to the Education Corps and two of them became my friends. One was very large, tall, overweight, wore thick glasses, and was called Trundle. The other was very thin, small and also bespectacled. They looked rather like an intellectual Laurel and Hardy together. We all disliked the barracks and used to sit in the NAAFI, gloomily soothing our wounded psyches with cups of tea and bitter sarcasm against the system.

The Army (in the upright shape of the PT sergeant) soon noticed that we three were physically unfit and unlikely to pass our Physical Efficiency Tests. These had to be passed before you could complete your basic training. If you did not qualify you had to do another eight weeks. I could see myself spending the two years endlessly sweating through the same basic training.

We could not climb ropes with speed. In fact, in my case, I could not climb ropes at all. I had a strong fear of heights and had no intention of leaving ground level. We also tended to slither over the vaulting box instead of lithely leaping over it. I had a long history of physical inactivity. Natural laziness at school had combined with maternal protectiveness to produce a creature that could walk or totter, but do little else. (My mother used to say, 'Why don't clergymen fall out of trees?' And answer, 'Because they don't climb them.') At school I had carefully avoided climbing trees or ropes or anything else that involved unnecessary risks. Even step ladders gave me vertigo. During games I had given an excellent imitation of someone who is keen but somehow finds himself a long way away from the action. It is no wonder I became a cartoonist: it is the ideal sedentary occupation. You might go mad, but you do not need to be physically brave.

The Army decided that we needed some extra help to complete our training, and we were sent on a special course for the physically inadequate held at the PT Depot, Shorncliffe, near Folkestone. Squads of weak-kneed,

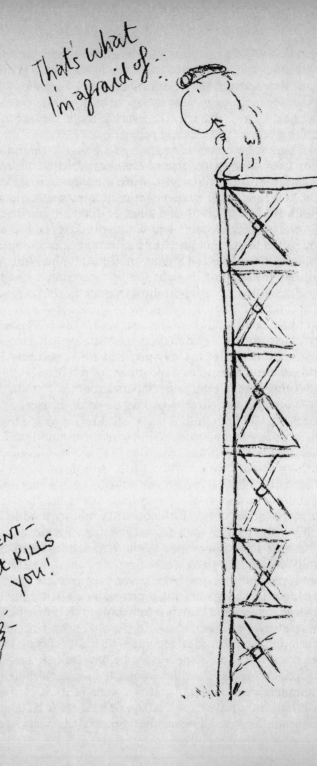

round-shouldered, skinny and fat misfits were gathered there and PT sergeants exhausted themselves trying to make men of us.

We went for long runs along the deserted beach in the morning. It was November and very cold. We had to go on long marches. And when we were not running or marching, we were doing PT.

Worst of all, we had special sessions called 'Confidence Training', which eroded what little confidence I had left. The climax of these sessions was a thirty-foot scaffolding, which we had to climb and then descend, from rung to rung. I managed to get up and at the top stopped to rest and shiver with fright on a tiny platform. Far below me, to the left, I could see the military hospital; to the right, the military cemetery. I thought this was carrying a joke too far. I tried to lower myself down and panic set my limbs into damp jelly. I could not move. I could hear faint shouts of encouragement from the PT sergeant below, but I could not unfix myself. I closed my eyes and sweated. Eventually the sergeant had to climb up, hold me round the waist, and lower me like a drunk down to ground level.

Of the three of us, one broke his leg whilst training his confidence and another had a nervous breakdown and was invalided out.

I returned alone to our unit, back to marching, drilling and bulling for eternity, as far as I could see, since I still had not learnt how to climb ropes. I always tried to run round the ropes when the sergeant was not looking.

But I was reprieved. Somewhere in the machinery, a faceless cog discovered that a potential education sergeant was taking twelve weeks to do his basic six weeks' training and posted me (still unconfident and unathletic) to the depot of the Education Corps.

6. Stand to attention when I'm educating you

The Depot was at Beaconsfield, close by the Tudor-beamed and dainty tea shops. It was still the Army, but the Army ever so slightly softened; I was still a private, but the vision of three stripes and my own room glowed like an icon amongst the heathen.

One night whilst on guard duty I vomited. My stomach (always a rather delicate organ, more suited to a retired lady living in Broadstairs than an Army segeant) had decided to revolt against the strong tea and greasy fried eggs. I reported sick the next morning, which meant packing your small kit (I do not know what happened if you were too sick to do this) with regulation pyjamas prs 1, soap 1, towel 1, vest 1, socks prs 1, PT shoes (for use as slippers), pants 1, and housewife. The MO listened with apathy and prescribed M & D (Medicine and Duties). I was told to watch my diet: drink milk instead of tea, he said. Yes, sir, I said.

Three times a day I had to go and collect my spoonful of chalky white medicine.

'I always drink some before I go on the booze,' said the medical orderly cheerfully. 'It lines your stomach.'

In the Army you were not allowed to keep a bottle, but had to report for each dose. This suited me, as it was a pleasant walk to the MO hut, and it wasted a half hour.

I decided to avoid as many meals as possible. Instead of greasy breakfasts I had some cream crackers I kept in my locker, and water. I did not have the courage to ask the cook for weak tea (I could see him recoiling) but had asked him for milk as per MO's orders and he had said no. I cannot remember why he refused, but as a private I had learned that asking 'why?' was not the best way to make friends.

It was now December, snow had fallen and it was very cold. I found the solitary breakfasts of crackers and water (some lucky mornings I managed to scrounge hot water) poor protection against the cold and my habitual melancholy. The Army on a full stomach was depressing enough, but on cream crackers it was suicidal. I had fantasies of deserting, but the thought of glasshouse food (being a natural pessimist, I knew I would be caught) stopped me.

As soon as my duties were over, I would leave the Depot and hurry to the local beamed teashop and gorge myself on poached eggs and toast and weak tea. I began to feel even more like an old lady and less like a soldier than ever.

Christmas was coming, the goose was getting fat and I was tucking into cream crackers and hot water. I prayed that God would try and do something about my stomach. I depended on God a great deal because I had realised that the MO was not very interested in my stomach. I do not know if it was God or the doses of Mag. Trisilicate but after a few weeks my stomach stopped aching and settled down to Army food again. But I continued to treat it with respect and vetted everything I sent down.

Whilst we learned to become sergeant/instructors we were watched to see if we were suitable NCO material. We knew the Army was short of education sergeants, so we assumed that we would all pass out, provided we did not strike anyone.

One morning all the names of the promoted privates were posted up on the notice board. Everyone's name was there except for mine and one other (and he was even more unlike a potential sergeant than I was).

The CO sent for me.

'I'm rather worried about you,' he said. 'We've been observing you and we feel you're not very happy in the Army.'

'Oh, no, sir,' I said, 'I've just got this miserable face. I can't help it. Even when I'm feeling very happy, I look gloomy.'

He looked unconvinced.

'You're not a Bolshie, are you?'

'Goodness, no, sir.' I desperately tried to think of something to convince him of my essential rightness as NCO material. My dreams of a room of my own were fading away.

'In fact, sir, before I joined the Army, I drew for *Punch*.' (I had drawn some very small headings for them but I did not think I needed to be too specific about the size at this moment.) 'Well, I wouldn't draw for *Punch* if I was a Bolshie, would I, sir?'

He smiled and leaned forward.

'Really . . . *Punch*, eh? You must do some jokes for us. Lots of material here . . . ha . . . ha . . . Well, that's all right, then. . . .'

And it was. The next day my promotion was announced in Part One orders and I was through to the splendours of sergeanthood and a room of my own.

I was posted as an education sergeant (my fresh white stripes glowing on my slightly grubby battledress) to the Depot of the Veterinary Corps.

'It's a tricky posting,' said the major, 'but you're resilient.'

Am I? I thought.

The Depot was in Melton Mowbray, where they make pies and pet food, surrounded by lovely countryside and posh people hunting foxes. The Depot trained men, horses and dogs. Mainly dogs and dog handlers; the horses were remnants of the past.

The sergeants' mess was a strange mixture of dog men and horse men, both groups always telling each other of the natural superiority of their own animals. The horse men were older and nicer; some remembered the cavalry. The dog men were tougher, more like policemen.

As I knew nothing about either dogs or horses, I found it difficult to enter into the conversations. Or what passed for conversation. The talk was ritualised into mocking, sneering, swearing and joking. The dog men sneered at the horse men for having a cushy life, whilst they did the real work. The horse men mocked the others for training dogs, whilst they handled the only intelligent creatures in the Depot, horses.

I was frightened of both the enormous horses and the enormous Alsatians, so I kept away from the working part of the Depot. I had a school room, a library and my own room in a hut at the far end of the Depot, and could retreat there and be forgotten.

I was called 'Schoolie', the traditional name for the education sergeant, which gives some indication of the contempt the subject was held in by the rest of the Army.

I was an ersatz sergeant. The rank was given for the sake

of discipline (instruction equals telling them equals rank) but everyone knew you had not earned the stripes the hard way. I was not a sergeant in my bones. I did not stand up straight; I tended to sag in the middle. My clothes were crumpled, no matter how often I ironed them. My brasses glowered rather than glowed, and there were always bits of dried Brasso visible on the matted green blanco. My hair was not worn as close to the skull as that of the other sergeants. I had no medals, I had fought no wars.

The real sergeants bored me, and I am sure I irritated them. The mess was claustrophobic. The same jokes, the same exchanges every day. One sergeant used to say to the mess waiter every night after supper, 'Serve the coffee in the drawing-room near the potted palms,' and laugh. He always called rice pudding 'Chinese wedding cake'. I used to tense myself, waiting for him to say, 'I'll have the Chinese wedding cake' and want to poison it. I used to eat quickly and escape as soon as possible.

It was like a soft prison; or an atheistic monastery.

I went to the cinema in Nottingham two or three times a week. I went to dances. I read like an addict. I wrote a little. I tried to do some cartoons for *Soldier* magazine, with some success.

I spent most of my service with the Veterinary Corps. It was my own fault that I learned nothing about animals, but I learned about people. I learned how to manage and tame the Army system. I learned how to avoid trouble.

I enjoyed teaching, organising the classes and cramming the soldiers through their Certificate of Education. The training officer and I made an unspoken pact. I would get the men their Certificates, and I would be allowed to go my own way.

I started a magazine for all the other education sergeants in North Midland District. It was mostly written by myself, and run off on an old duplicator, but I did not care. It helped to keep me from falling fast asleep.

I started a film society at the camp because I wanted to see some old films from the British Film Institute, and a small huddle of soldiers who were broke and could not afford to go into Nottingham would come once a fortnight and see Buster Keaton and two free films from the Shell Film Unit.

I tried to encourage some of my pupils to read the books

in the unit library, but soon gave up evangelical work as too difficult and irrelevant to their lives. I learned a lot about the problems of communicating with people: I remember spending ten minutes discussing, 'Should Capital Punishment be Abolished?' and then reading in one soldier's essay, 'Capital punishment should not be abolished. It should be made stricter.'

I used to get up too late for breakfast, so illicitly cooked for myself in my room on a tiny hotplate which I ran off the lamp. The same heater helped to warm the wooden room in winter. I had a large adapter on the lamp, so I could have a radio, light and hotplate all on at the same time. I made tea and boiled eggs every morning until I fused all the lights, and someone got suspicious, and I had to give up cooked breakfasts.

Usually I rose only fifteen minutes before my first class at nine o'clock. A quick shave, wash, dress and next door to work.

One morning I woke at eight-thirty and was lying on the bed, thinking about getting up, when there was a loud knocking on the door. Having learnt to be cautious, I didn't shout 'fuck off', but lay still. The knocking continued louder and an officer-class voice shouted:

'Are you there, sergeant?' I carefully got up, crept to the door, and looked through the keyhole. There was the District Education Officer, on a surprise inspection visit.

I did not think he would appreciate being greeted by an undressed, unshaven education sergeant, so I froze. More banging, more shouting. More trying the door handle. Fortunately I always kept the door locked at night. At last he stamped off.

I dressed, rushed out to the washroom to shave, cut myself, rushed back to my room, picked up some books to look busy, and then walked as calmly as I could across the parade ground. The officer was at the far end just by the adjutant's office.

'Sergeant!' he shouted.

'Good morning, sir,' I said.

'Where have you been? I tried your room. I tried the library.'

He seemed annoyed.

'I was in the cookhouse, sir, putting up some posters for my next film show.'

I hoped he would not go and see them, because they were not there.

'Well, sergeant, come and show me your school room. You should be in your library at this time.'

He was very keen, so I did not like to tell him that I only loaned out two books a week, and certainly none at nine o'clock in the morning.

The Army was an education. It helped me to find myself in ways that I never had at art school. Being in an alien group made me define my own boundaries. At art school, at home, always surrounded by sympathetic, nice, liberal people, I had merged with them and never discovered my identity. Here, amongst all the fuck me, fuck you, fuck the expense, give the cat a goldfish, I felt more myself.

There was 'them' and there was 'me'. They spoke a language that said 'cunt' instead of 'woman' and 'fuck' instead of 'love'. A landscape that was only straight lines. A country where it was virtue not to think, not to use your imagination. If it stands still, paint it; if it moves, salute it; if it thinks, bellow at it.

I knew I was different and accepted it. At school I had felt different as a Jew, and had felt uneasy about it. Here, I was different and thanked God for it. I did not want to be a real sergeant. I was disguised as one and counted the days when I could shed the disguise and get on with my real life.

7. A short-sighted approach to Miles Davis

As soon as I came out of the Army in 1956 I went out looking for freelance work. My folder was on the slim side: two book jackets and a mixture of (mostly unpublished) small black-and-white humorous illustrations.

I called on everyone I could think of – magazines, book publishers and advertising agencies. I tried to get an agent but no one would have me. I realised that I needed to create my own markets, and called on magazines that did not use illustration. I reckoned that there would be less competition there and that the more staid the magazine, the more likely they were to need visual leavening.

One of my first clients was nearly blind but I don't like to think that had anything to do with my getting the commission. My friend, Kitty, worked for Carlo Kramer who ran Esquire Records from his basement flat in Bedford Square. She knew that I badly needed work to fill out my emaciated folder and kindly gave me a record sleeve to design. It was a record by Miles Davis (one of his first classics, with John Coltrane). I had never heard Miles before so she played me the record.

The music was strange and beautiful and I tried – very inadequately – to capture this feeling in the design. Two weeks later I brought her the rough sketch and we went to show it to Mr Kramer.

It was a slightly unnerving experience. He held the drawing right up against his one good eye, so that he looked like a jeweller examining a rare diamond, whilst Kitty described the details.

'There's a tree on the left and some clouds in the sky and the lettering is in red . . .' When she had finished talking, Mr Kramer sighed and vaguely nodded agreement. 'If you like it, Kitty . . .'

I was rather proud of the finished design and for a long time carried it around in my folder. I also enjoyed illicitly listening to the record. I say 'illicitly' because Mr Kramer felt the fee of five guineas was more than enough without

giving me the record as well – and Kitty had to extract the copy for me when he wasn't looking. . . .

Not all my clients were physically handicapped. George Scott, who edited *Truth* magazine, was in robust good health and gave me a lot of work. *Truth* was a rather idiosyncratic journal that nourished maverick writers. I drew regularly for them and also contributed to their Diary column.

I slowly evolved a personal approach to illustration and it became less of a sweat and more of a pleasure. I could always tell how much I liked doing a job by the amount of process white I used: the more white used, the more hateful the work.

I met some resistance. One art director, Lewis Carroll, (of Macmillan) suggested I go to art school.

'I've been to art school,' I said.

'Good God,' he said, 'What on earth do they teach there these days?'

I muttered something about drawing.

'Drawing,' he snorted. 'You can't draw. Look at this man.' He picked up a large colour proof of the House of Commons drawn in amazingly boring detail by someone whose name escapes me. 'See that. You can recognise every Member of Parliament there. That's what I call Drawing. Study that and try to draw like that. Then I might be able to give you some work. . . .'

Another art director (of *Illustrated* magazine) nearly reduced me to tears by saying that I was wasting my time and ought to find another way to earn a living.

Eventually I learned the knack of having at least two appointments a day, so that if one was too truthful and unkind, the other might be tactful and encouraging.

One lady was encouraging. She was Pat McNeill, assistant art editor of *Woman* magazine. She had no work for me, but she laughed at my jokes and I was so grateful that I ended up marrying her. But that is another story.

I showed my folder to Christian Barman, a sort of advertising guru, who said that my work was individual. 'There's no middle ground for work like that. You'll either succeed or fail utterly.'

That was a remark I treasured and would often repeat it to myself when I was getting discouraged.

8. Add a pinch of Steinberg . . .

In order to write this book I have been sorting out some of the drawings I have done in the past thirty years or so. I keep finding odd scribbles that I thought I had thrown out. Their only interest is that they remind me of the long, slow process of learning how to be a cartoonist. It is all trial and error. I must have drawn hundreds of drawings before I slowly developed a style that could convey what I wanted to say. It is not an overnight process.

I remember wanting desperately to think of funny situations and lines and failing. I could not find the key to the 'joke' section of my brain. I would dream up a small gag and then agonise over it – drawing it and redrawing it until it lost any spontaneity it once had. There is one cartoon I did, whilst in the Army, that I kept reworking. I illustrate two versions here.

'Now write out one hundred times, "I must not bring my guard dog into Education Classes." '

So there were two separate problems: thinking up jokes and then drawing them succinctly to extract the maximum flavour and zest from the idea. Ideas did not lead on to other ideas. I did not know how to let the mind relax and wander by association from notion to notion. I still do not understand why this process becomes easier with practice, but it does. Thank God.

I reproduce some of these early drawings, these painful attempts at humour, to show how inept I was. I often experimented with different styles in a vain hope that I would stumble on the perfect style.

I sold some drawings to *Soldier* magazine whilst in the Army and learned a great deal from seeing my drawings in print. There is some mysterious thing that happens to your work when it is printed: you can see exactly what is wrong (or right) with it. All its faults become glaringly obvious. It is like seeing one's own child outside the home – you suddenly realise that what seemed clever and smart is rather precocious and awful.

I was also trying to find my own voice. I was heavily influenced by the many cartoonists I admired. Thurber, of course. And Steinberg – more for his thinking than for his graphic style. I also absorbed some aspects of Jules Feiffer. He proved a mixed blessing because I was soon bogged down in trying to write long captions in his manner. It did not suit me and only led to more despair.

'*I do wish someone would come and introduce us.*'

'Room service please.'

'I never saw such a man for his morning paper.'

9. A real job in upper and lower case

As well as my freelance work as a cartoonist/illustrator, I found a daytime job, as the assistant to a designer/typographer, Alec Davis. He was a nice, kind man who specialised in what was then called 'house style' and is now known as 'corporate image'. It is all about the overall look of a company: its letterheads, its signs, its trucks, the whole way it presents itself to the outside world. It has now become a very big business but was then a small, somewhat under-appreciated affair.

I worked at first in Alec Davis's office and I was very flustered by feeling that he was watching me all the time. I would throw away all my bungled layouts when he was out of the office, so that he would not see how inept I was. I had picked up some crumbs of typographical knowledge from various sources but I had not yet learned how to assemble them into a proper loaf of edible bread.

I had never worked for a designer before and had no idea of how obsessively tidy designers are. A desire for order is presumably what motivates them to become designers in the first place – but they carry this compulsion into everyday life. I have never been very tidy and was puzzled by Alec's constant throwing away of anything that cluttered up his desk. Equally, he was irritated by the state of my dishevelled desk.

After a few months, I was given a room of my own and this helped our relationship no end.

Later on in life, I shared an office with two designers and one of them, Graham Bishop, was visibly distressed by the condition of my desk. 'Please try to tidy up your desk,' he would beg every day. The clutter agitated him, whilst it soothed me. The sight of a bare desk fills me with terror – I am compelled to spread papers all over it before I can work.

I can enter a virgin hotel room and within hours make it look as if I've lived in it for years. It's a gift, I guess.

I once ate a sandwich lunch with a designer friend and I

saw her shudder when I threw my greasy wrapping paper into her white wastepaper basket. This same friend also spent a happy weekend, *washing* her book covers so that they looked fresh for her new office. They're a funny lot.

Anyway – back to Alec Davis. He was a very conscientious designer and deliberated and fretted over every tiny detail. I was impatient and eager to finish a job, whilst he loved endlessly changing and fine-tuning. (I think that my impatience has made me ideal cannon fodder for newspaper editors – they need everything yesterday.)

Alec taught me to recognise and understand the ingredients of good typography. Something of his own attitudes rubbed off on to me, so that today I know what I should be doing, even if I often fail to do it. I do try to take care of the small details that make all the difference between a mediocre job and a good one.

This attention to detail is important in book-jacket design. The space is very small, and the jacket is like a miniature poster. The information (title, author, flavour of the book) has to be conveyed simply and quickly. The potential buyer has to be intrigued and beguiled into picking up the book and then, one hopes, buying the book. Most publishers try to do too much in this small space and the result is usually an almighty mess.

(Of course, one doesn't always please. I remember designing a jacket with Philip Thompson, and the author wrote to us saying that he hated the map we'd used, he hated my drawing, he hated the lack of relevant photographs – and the only thing he did like was the use of white space. . . .)

After I had spent a long year with Alec Davis, the fiddling nature of the work began to bore me and I noticed that I was taking longer and longer lunch hours – always a bad sign. So I quit.

'Perhaps your talents are more graphic than typographic,' Alec said, making one of his rare jokes, when I told him that I was leaving.

I don't think real work suits me . .

10. Hold the front page – I'm just finishing my inch-high drawing

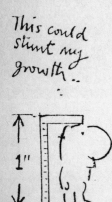

This could stunt my growth..

1"

My first newspaper job was with the *Daily Express*. I had written to them when I left art school and was eventually hired by Harold Keeble to illustrate the William Hickey column. I was so excited by this chance to work in Fleet Street that when they asked me to start the next week I was too overawed to mention that I was getting married on that day. So I got married in the morning and went along to the *Express* after the wedding celebration lunch.

In fact, I need not have been so keen, because no one knew what to do with me and I went home after an hour's hanging around downstairs in the lobby. The next day I went on my honeymoon and hoped that this golden opportunity would not evaporate in the meantime.

When I really began, I went in every evening around five o'clock, read all the Hickey stories as they were written and then chose one or two items to illustrate. They were not really cartoons – more humorous drawings with some visual twist added. There was no room for words or captions. As they had to be small (rarely deeper than 1½ inches by a single column) I had to learn how to compress a great deal into a tiny space.

I learned the virtues of economy. I learned how to think and draw very quickly; everything seemed to be in a hurry. There was rarely time to look up a picture reference, so I had to use and develop my memory. I slowly built up a cartoon vocabulary, so that I could express a shorthand version of almost anything I wanted to draw. I learned the difference between drawing for oneself (as I did as a student) and communicating with other people.

I also learned the value of persistence. For the first two weeks my drawings never appeared in the paper. Every morning I would rush downstairs to grab the *Express*, turn to the Hickey page and there was this terrible lack of Calman. My career appeared to be over before it had even begun. I finally summoned up the courage to ask what was wrong.

Enquiries were made and the answer was simple: the sub-editor who put the page together had not been told about my drawings and so had not allowed room for them on his layouts. It was my first important lesson in the problems of communication in the communications business.

The *Daily Express* was then a rather glamorous paper and some of the best-known names in popular journalism worked for it: Giles, Osbert Lancaster, Anne Scott-James, Drusilla Beyfus, Eve Perrick, Tony Armstrong-Jones, Robb, John French and many others.

Donald Edgar edited the Hickey Diary, with the help of a small team. He was flamboyant in manner and rather intimidated me. I always imagined that he had seen too many movies about newspapers and had decided to act the part to the hilt. He even sometimes wore his hat in the office as if he were auditioning for a role in *The Front Page*. He did write effectively . . . with a great flourish of dots . . . like this . . . to help the atmosphere along. . . .

I loved going in every night. I relished the noise of people typing, telephones ringing, the hurry and bustle, the deadlines, the sense of being in the centre of things (actually something of an illusion as I later discovered), the feeling of drama that newspaper men and women love to generate. Even the lines of newspaper vans waiting in the side streets for the finished copies excited me. I remember once telling a friend proudly that I now worked for the *Express* and he replied, 'Is that the Express Dairy?'

One of my great pleasures was watching Osbert Lancaster work. He had such style. He seemed so much at ease – never flustered or panic-stricken. Whilst I agonised over my little bits and pieces he would stroll in, read the papers, chat to friends, wander about, settle down, shoot his starched cuffs a few times, stroke his impressive moustache, draw his cartoon and suavely disappear into the night. I wanted to be like him more than anyone else on the paper; he was the essence of wit and urbanity. I was too shy ever to talk to him, apart from the occasional 'good evening' when we passed each other in the corridors.

It always amused me when I would take my tiny offering along to the picture desk and there see the process man measuring up Osbert's cartoon, rubbing out the

Illustrations to William Hickey diary. *Daily Express*: 1957–62

SUCCESS !

THANKS to the sacrifice of 62 Canadian bears, 124 of the Guardsmen who stand sentry duty outside Buckingham Palace will be snugly, and smartly, bearskinned from now on.

That famous bear hunt at Timmins in Ontario, organised when local hunters heard the

guards needed new headgear, has come to a close with a 62-strong bag.

Future supplies should be assured. The Mayor of Timmins, **Leo Del Villano**, said yesterday that many of those who took part in the hunt

PROGRESS

I HEAR that **Lord Tredegar** is racing around the Norwegian fiords in one of those new jet speedboats.

That's a far cry from the days when his ancestor languished in

the doldrums, waiting for a wind to push him along. For Lord Tredegar is descended from Henry Morgan, the buccaneer.

INCONVENIENT

SIR DUDLEY CUNLIFFE-OWEN, 35, has returned from his month-long holiday cruise. And yesterday he was in no mood to talk about it.

His 53ft. yacht Maudralic had broken down twice with engine

trouble, once at Rouen, again at Paris.

"It was merely," said Sir Dudley stiffly, "inconvenient."

JUBILANT

MR. JULIO LOBO, the Cuban sugar magnate who spends so much of his time gathering items for his

Napoleonic museum, has reached London from Paris jubilant at his latest acquisition.

It is Napoleon's toothbrush.

BUT, WHERE ?

IN full dress uniform, complete with shining spurs, **Major-General Brian Daunt** (hobbies : fishing, hunting, shooting, climbing, ski-ing, sailing and polo) flew to Exeter from London yesterday with the **Princess Royal** to inspect the Royal Corps of Signals, Junior Leaders' Regiment, at Newton Abbot, Devon.

As General Daunt boarded the Royal Flight passengers

from a Comet just in from New York passed by.

And a young boy was heard to ask his father : "Gee, dad, where would he park his horse around here ? "

THEIR POND

GOT a problem ? Then take it to the Territorial Association. That most versatile of organisations seems to have the answer to most things—even to the request of

the fly fishermen of England for a suitable pond to cast on.

This came from the Country Landowners' Association who are organising a Gamefair in

FROM THE SHAH

THERE is a new Persian carpet in Buckingham Palace. It was the Shah's present to the Queen, given to her on the day before his state visit to Britain ended.

The carpet, which measures 8ft. by 12ft., is a decided cut

above the sort of thing you will find in the best of furnishing stores.

It was specially made for the Queen by Persian craftsmen who wove some 1,000 stitches into every square inch.

the only dog which eats regularly out of a Sevres bowl. She and her family eat off Sevres too, for she believes that it is pointless to hoard things away unseen."

What does Lady Elizabeth, the Marquis of Anglesey's sister, think of this tribute ?

"It's quite undeserved," she tells me. "There isn't a piece of

Sevres in the house. There are two dogs, though. One has a bowl marked Dog, and the other eats out of the handiest kitchen plate."

pencil drawing that still showed underneath the finished penwork, muttering, 'dirty bugger, dirty bugger'. Not a word about the witty line or caption – just this complaint about the obtrusive pencil marks. It told me so much about the nature of working for newspapers. I soon learned that what most sub-editors cared about was the size of my drawing. Was it too big? The content was rarely commented on.

This same man also checked Giles's cartoon every night. I watched him scanning the drawing very carefully and asked him why he gave it this careful scrutiny.

'Giles once sneaked in a packet of Durex right on the back shelf of one of his crowded shop scenes and since then I check every inch of his cartoons.' And he laughed affectionately.

I worked at the *Express* for over five years, until 1963. During that time I also illustrated the letters page, features, gardening columns, book reviews, travel articles – almost everything apart from the crossword puzzle and the astrology column.

The trouble with being expert at drawing small cartoons was that I was offered other work involving drawing small cartoons. I wanted to develop and realised that if I did not leave the *Express* I would be doing the same work for the rest of my days. There was no ladder of ascent at the *Express*; I could not slowly climb from apprentice to front-page cartoonist. The existing cartoon stars were in their firmament and likely to remain so until the end of time.

I was bored reading the same gossip stories about errant debutantes eloping with well-bred cads, and then trying to do one-inch drawings about them. I knew I had to move on.

Never mind the joke – feel the depth . . .

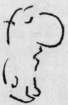

11. *Tonight* and every night

Once I had decided, in 1963, to leave the *Daily Express*, I had to find something else to do. I very much wanted a change from newspapers and thought I would see if I could get involved with television in some way. I had read that the BBC TV programme *Tonight*, which was a highly successful topical news programme, was about to have a new editor, Peter Batty, and so I wrote to him, asking if he wanted a cartoonist.

Peter was interested in the idea and offered me a four-week trial, going in every night and illustrating (off-camera) light-hearted items. Every afternoon I went to their small studios in Lime Grove and learned how to work for this very different medium.

There were a few minor technical differences. Pens and pencils were too thin to be effective, so I had to use thick magic markers, which were bolder but also less subtle. I also had to draw on thick grey cards, as white dazzled the cameras. The drawings were then propped up before the cameras and video-recorded for transmission that evening.

I learnt that the drawings were seen as a sequence, and that you could make a humorous point by placing one drawing against another. It was like a basic form of film editing. I also discovered that it was more effective if the camera moved across the drawing. Even a simple zoom-in to a 'close-up' of a detail made the drawing come alive. The eye of the viewer is so used to constant movement on television that any static shots look dull.

It also became clear that TV devours material. For a short four-minute item, I would need to draw about ten to fifteen drawings. I would spend all afternoon working on the drawings and then see them disappear in the blink of an eye.

It was, however, exciting to work at such pressure, as every item was conceived and produced the same day. It was also more of a collaboration than newspaper work, where I simply did my drawing and handed it over to the process department. Here, I was involved with the script and could suggest ideas for items.

I was always looking for ways to get out of the studios and into the real world. I easily became bored with sitting alone in a room with a pencil – and still do.

So I suggested that I should be allowed to cover various seasonal events with a tape recorder and sketchbook. We evolved a method that worked very well. I went to the event (the Chelsea Flower Show, for instance) and chatted to people, recording their reactions and sometimes eaves-dropping on their conversation. I also sketched my impressions of the scene. I then returned to the studios where we edited down the material into a sound track of about four to five minutes long. I would illustrate this sound track with my drawings and suggest various camera movements across them. The whole thing was then video-taped.

I once managed to go to the Royal Academy Summer Exhibition Private View in the morning, edit the tape, do the drawings and finish the item in time for transmission that evening at six o'clock.

I was shy at first about going up to people and asking them questions, but I soon learned to overcome that feeling. I also had the good advice and help of the BBC sound recordists who came with me. They were always patient, calm and willing to take endless trouble to get the right effect.

One, in particular, Don Martin, had worked with Alan Whicker a great deal and taught me something of the skills of sound interviewing. He explained to me the art of nodding agreement instead of saying 'Yes, yes'. The nodding of the head does not appear on the sound track and therefore does not confuse the final editing. There is nothing more annoying than trying to cut a sentence and finding that one's own voice, saying something unnecess-ary like 'Oh, really', prevents a neat edit.

I enjoyed the pleasure of working with professionals – everyone was eager to make the programme as good as it could possibly be. *Tonight* occupied a unique place then in viewers' affections and this knowledge contributed to the quality of the programme.

There was also the very trivial but undeniable pleasure

of 'fame-by-TV-association'. I remember going to my regular garage one day, for some routine service call, and being treated with new respect. Suddenly the hitherto reticent assistant was very talkative. 'What's it like, then, on *Tonight?* What is Cliff Michelmore *really* like?' He had seen my name on the closing credits and even though I was a minor cog in the television wheel, I had acquired some new status in his eyes. And whenever I phoned in future, he was always warm and welcoming: 'Hello, Mr Calman – and how are *you* today?' It was as if I had changed my humble Morris Minor for a Rolls Royce.

12. How to oil the creative wheels with a 4B pencil

One client found me, which made a pleasant change. Most of my life in those days was spent looking for clients. Arthur Wilson, as art director at Mather and Crowther (now Ogilvy and Mather), working on the Shell account, had noticed my little drawings in the William Hickey column and thought that I had ideas above my graphic station. He phoned me and asked me to come round and talk to him.

Arthur was a jolly, energetic, enthusiastic man who had this strange faith in my ability to produce ideas. He used a cunning mixture of praise and scorn ('Come on, Mel, you can do better than that') to goad and coax me into doing work that I didn't know I could do. Of course, that is what a good art director should do, but there are very few such people around.

We formed a team of four – Arthur, Paul Hoppe (a very sharp-witted, sharp-tongued copywriter), Maurice Smelt (a kind, highly intelligent group copy head) and myself – and we worked very amicably together. We would meet regularly for a sandwich lunch and dream up themes for campaigns. We were given a great deal of freedom by the client and often used seasonal and topical events as springboards for advertisements. We all liked working quickly and produced topical ads at great speed. Even the Denning Report had our Shell comment in the newspapers on the day it was published.

We devised a 'Shell Guide to the Affluent Society' for a series of ads for the new *Sunday Times Colour Magazine*.

At first I had severe problems working in these bigger spaces after the single-column drawings of the *Daily Express*. We experimented with different techniques; at that time I used an old-fashioned fountain pen (which never left my side) and the line it produced was rather thin and under-nourished. I tried different pens – Arthur even made me try quill pens and the sharpened wrong end of a dip pen. We finally settled on a soft pencil (4B or 5B). The

Plate I

The Spreading Parking Meter

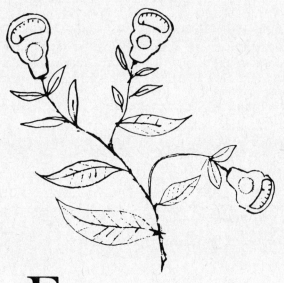

EXCLUSIVELY a town plant.
Originally cultivated for usefulness.
Multiplies overnight, often found
where least expected. Grows to some
4-ft., sturdy stem. Yields daily harvest.
Feed with small coin regularly.
Do not overfeed. Fast becoming
almost as common as the Shell sign,
but not nearly so popular.

The Other Driver

Me

I am the careful driver

 I never disconcert you

  My car is full of Super Shell

   And I am full of virtue

He is the Other Driver

 And it's strange to think that he

  A patent rogue and menace

   Thinks just the same of me

MORAL: All Other Drivers' habits are very hard to tell
But (like the Other Driver) you can be sure of Shell

line was thicker and more interesting, but, more important, I felt more relaxed using a pencil. It was more like 'play' and less like proper artwork.

Most people become inhibited when they try to draw carefully, so the trick is to be as relaxed as possible, whilst still keeping the adrenalin necessary to stimulate ideas. Perhaps that is why I leave everything to the last minute. Panic certainly ensures that the adrenalin levels are nicely topped up.

The Shell campaigns lasted for over three years until Esso opened up the door to a harder-sell approach to petrol advertising with their 'Tiger' ads. Shell abandoned humour and began tearing up bank notes. Petrol stations gave away halves of token notes and customers advertised in the personal columns of *The Times*: 'Half of £100 note wishes to meet another'.

I was very sorry – and so was my bank manager. A charming tradition, which stretched back to the Thirties, of using artists like Edward Bawden, Brian Robb, Ben Nicholson, McKnight Kauffer and Paul Nash had ended.

13. Dial a book

When I was thirty, I decided that I must try and produce a book of my own. I had illustrated other people's work for so long that I was frightened that I would never venture out on my own. I kept starting books and then abandoning them. My desk drawer was full of unfinished books, ideas that had seemed promising yet died prematurely.

We (my wife, Pat, and our new daughter, Stephanie) had recently moved into a flat in Bloomsbury and had inherited the last tenant's telephone directories. Three of them were in reasonable condition but the fourth one had been ravaged by the builders who had done the conversion. They had obviously run out of toilet paper and had used half the pages for a purpose totally unconnected with telephonic communication. Since I hate throwing anything away, I kept coming across this torn directory and brooded about its comic possibilities, if any.

One morning, I cut up some of the entries and collaged them into a handful of cartoons. I began with the instructions: 'Say who you are – do not say just "hello"' which showed a man reading out an extract from *Who's Who*. In those days, the exchanges had names instead of only numbers – and PRImrose, MAYfair etc. suggested other jokes. I cut up several entries and tried out different approaches – sometimes graphic, sometimes surreal.

I began confidently but after a day or two ran out of steam. I'd work and then cry out to Pat: 'It's no good, there are no more jokes about telephones.'

'Never mind,' she'd say soothingly, 'have a cup of tea and keep trying.' Or she would suggest a joke that seemed so awful that it goaded me to try and improve on it.

I would have abandoned this book, as I had the others, if I hadn't met Jonathan Clowes, who was Len Deighton's agent. Len had just acquired this brand-new agent to handle his first book, *The Ipcress File*.

Jonathan was a rather unusual agent; instead of having conventional offices in Mayfair or Bloomsbury, he worked from his small flat in Kentish Town. He had become an agent by chance and approached the task with all the energy and guile of a complete innocent. He once told me that he coped with film producers by saying nothing – and this always led to them raising their offers. He had only the one suit – a brown corduroy one that made him look like an out-of-work Fabian lecturer.

Anyway – I told Len of my telephone book idea and he advised me – no, instructed me, since Len was always convinced that he was right – to show the cartoons to Jonathan. He liked them and soon found a publisher for me. To my amazement I eventually had a proper contract for a book of cartoons. Here, at last, was my *first* book – all because I hadn't been able to throw out a half-torn telephone directory.

Every day I grappled with this theme and cudgelled my brains to squeeze one more joke out of the directory. I began to discover how to tease ideas out of the material. I tried to stop that awful inhibition that suffocates ideas before they can be given a chance to breathe. I allowed myself to freewheel so that a joke could surprise me by happening almost without my thinking about it. I didn't realise, of course, that I was doing all these things at the time – all I knew was that I was desperate to finish the book.

To look back at this book now is a curious experience. It is as if it had been drawn by someone else – the style seems so stiff and unwieldy. I used a pen then and that produced a stiffer line than a pencil does. But I like some of the cartoons – especially the more surreal ones. I like the name-droppers, the numbers bursting out of the wires, the numbers no longer available (on gravestones), and the numbers escaping from the handset to pursue the

'May I suggest the TRAfalgar 1860, sir?'

customer.

At last I had enough material for a slim volume and I felt an enormous sense of achievement. Whatever the book's faults and lacks, I had at last finished something.

And then a worrying thought disturbed my peace of mind. Wasn't the telephone directory Crown copyright? Did I need permission to use the material? I asked a solicitor friend who worked for the GPO, who said that the Post Office would never give permission for such *lèse-majesté*, and that I had better not ask. 'Just hope that no one notices your book,' he said.

The book was published, for some reason, in August, and the news of this event therefore appeared to have been embargoed under the Official Secrets Act. I was never sued by the Post Office. For several months friends would say to me, 'When is your book coming out?' and I would reply, 'It came out. You must have been away. People talk of little else.'

14. Room to let: would suit balding gentleman

The *Sunday Telegraph* started in 1962 and Jonathan Clowes told me that they were looking for a single-column cartoon for their diary page. I spent several days trying out various ideas and stumbled on the notion of a man living alone in a bed-sit. I did a cartoon of him about to enter the room, saying, 'It may be small but the proportions are pleasing.' Suddenly, he seemed a real person, as if I now had this friend who could say some of the things I thought and felt. He had a tone of voice that I could recognise and understand.

His views and opinions coincided in many ways with mine, but where I would be angry, he preferred to shrug his shoulders and mutter some wry aphorism. He was mild-mannered but quietly determined not to let life get

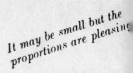

It may be small but the proportions are pleasing

the better of him.

At first, when he became a tenant in the feature, 'Bed-Sit', in the *Sunday Telegraph*, he only had opinions about his own life, but when he left the *Sunday Telegraph* and wandered over to *The Sunday Times* (via a short detour to *The Observer*), he had to become interested in the larger world outside his own head.

Since 1962 he has changed. He always looked middle-aged but he now really is middle-aged. His profile is more relaxed, less tense and his clothes have become loose lines that could be half garment, half body. He has a female companion who often seems to be rather cross about something. She looks very like him, except for the curly hair and dress. I notice that at various times in my life the woman is larger than the man – which I'm sure has some psychological significance that I would rather not know about.

He is my alter-ego: I don't know what I would do without him. I imagine that he feels the same way about me.

Which is it to be today?
Toast and music,
toast and light,
music and toast in
darkness,
toast in silence?

15. Business News and *Couples*

In the mid-Sixties I was drawing regularly for *The Sunday Times*. Every week I illustrated Business News articles and tried to find humour in the nooks and crannies of pension schemes, life assurance and death duties. I soon realised that I would never understand high finance and that the way to survive was to work at a slight tangent to the material. I tried to decipher what the technicalities boiled down to in simple terms and then make a joke out of that.

As a change from these financial cartoons I produced a series of features of my own. There was 'My God', then 'The Resident', which was an extension of 'Bed-Sit'. His philosophical aphorisms were rather downbeat, perhaps too downbeat for the Sixties, for his tenancy was rather brief.

A lot depends on timing in humour and my wry and slightly sceptical views are probably more suited to the present day.

A strip called 'Couples' ran for several months. This was an attempt to explore the gap between what people say and what they think. The top half showed a couple talking and the bottom half their private thoughts. I got the idea from seeing some strips by George Herriman, an American cartoonist, who had (in the early 1900s) created a double strip, about a cat and mouse living underneath a family, called 'The Dingbat Family'. (Eventually the family were evicted and the strip became 'Krazy Kat', to my mind the most original and brilliant comic strip ever.)

I have always been interested in the difference between thoughts and speech and a two-level strip seemed the best way to explore this division. I placed the thoughts on the bottom level so that they would be read after the spoken words. I considered drawing the bottom level as a surreal landscape – but that was too complicated.

I enjoyed doing this strip and I still think that it was the most interesting thing I did in those years. However, the editor of the 'Look' pages, Peter Crookston, thought that

Your Money and You: By Oliver Stanley

Double trouble

I'd like to keep a few crumbs for myself...

calman

country. There is a certain wild logic in this rule, for it leaves you to bear world tax at the higher of the two rates. Difficulties follow....

There is the task of finding what is the foreign rate. Up to April 6 last, you were often entitled to include not only tax directly withheld from dividends, but also that suffered by the company profits out of which the dividend had been paid—*indirect* tax. This relief, unilaterally given on Commonwealth country dividends, has now been withdrawn as conflicting with the principle of separating companies' and shareholders' liabilities. F u t u r e treaties will not include it for individual shareholders. For corporate shareholders the relief might be regarded as now tapering off, with a distinction between portfolio investment and investment in foreign subsidiaries. It is of course the latter which is favoured.

Next, you have to decide what is your relevant U K rate. This has always been the average

position of being unable to calculate the credit until having settled the reduced amount of dividend to be assessed. At the same time, we cannot settle the assessment until having fixed the credit. To escape from this vicious circle you have to rely on an arithmetical trick— "grossing up." Grossing up means finding the amount, which, after charge at the effective rate would produce the original dividend less foreign tax. If you prefer, it is the net dividend plus the credit on it

need to make on a yield basis to find the true net return on overseas investment. Suppose these figures represented a yield of 4 per cent. on £10,000. Then the true net is 2.2 per cent. as against 2.35 per cent. on a comparable U K investment. There is a distinct loss, but not so much as if you overlooked your D T R claim altogether.

At present there are prospects of improvement—and the reverse. From some future date

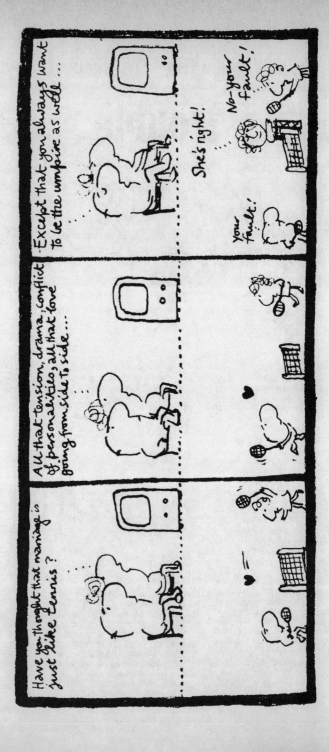

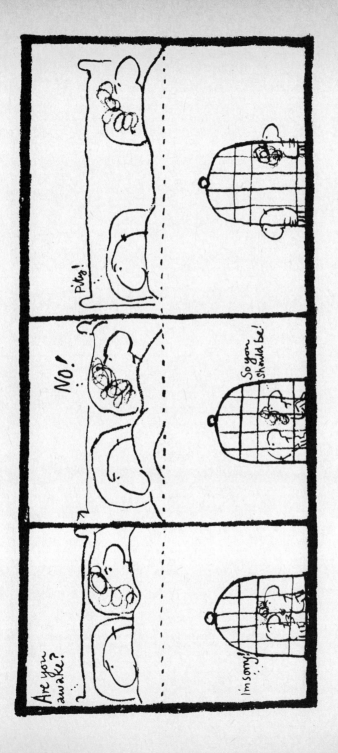

it was too complex and space-consuming. It travelled from page to page: Gardening to Letters to Fashion, everyone eager for someone else to have the honour of its glowing presence.

Then one week, without warning, it disappeared completely. I was very disgruntled and went to complain to the editor of *The Sunday Times*. I felt like a schoolboy. 'Please sir, it's not fair, sir . . .' Harry Evans was patient but preoccupied.

'Can't I have my own little corner somewhere?' I begged. 'A space I can call my own.'

Harry thought for a moment and then, more (I'm sure) to get rid of me than for any other reason, said, 'Why not do a topical cartoon every week – on the front page?'

'Fine,' I said, without thinking. 'When?'

'Start this week. I'll need it by Friday,' he said and then turned away to dictate memos in all directions.

Elation was followed by something close to panic. Up to then I had mostly made jokes about myself and my inner view of the world. I knew a great deal about the inside of my head but not very much about the political world outside it.

28 DECEMBER 1980

THE SUN

Perhaps the new 10/- piece looks like the 2/- one because that's what it's worth...

From *The Sunday Times* October 1969.

On Friday I sat down to gather my thoughts on the week's events. By the end of the day I had a head full of ungathered thoughts and a waste-paper basket full of torn paper. I finally produced a cartoon on the new fifty-pence coin that had just been launched. The cartoon may not seem very funny today but it turned out to be prophetic.

From then on it became a little easier every week, although doing a weekly cartoon is, I think, harder than a daily one. If you have several shots at a target you can score a few misses without anyone noticing but if you have only the one arrow then it had better score a bull's eye.

I produced this weekly cartoon, rain or shine, through marriage and divorce, for fourteen years. And then one day in 1983, I was telephoned by the managing editor and informed that the new editor, Andrew Neil, did not think that my cartoons were funny. So I left *The Sunday Times*. I waited for the postman to bring bags of letters from deprived readers, saying that a light had gone out of their lives. None arrived. I expect everyone was too upset to put pen to paper.

Harry Evans, when he was editor of The Sunday Times, *had the virtue of knowing when to say 'yes'. There is nothing better than an editor who says 'yes' to your ideas instead of 'yes-but'. On several occasions I suggested doing cartoons in unusual ways – in one instance, across the top of the front and back pages, and he always responded with enthusiasm.*

No 8166   Price   30p

AY TIMES

ll prevail.
will LOVE JEW,
SSIAN LOVE
AMERICAN,
Irishman
Love
RISHMAN...

A marshmallow
softness
will pervade
MANKIND—
Even GASMEN
will turn up at
the APPOINTED
HOUR...

Thinks:
IS this
TRUE?

NO!
But who wants
depressing
predictions
at a time like
this?

16. *Nova* and *Town*

Many years ago, before he discovered the joys of wearing flak jackets, Michael Heseltine published (with Clive Labovitch) a man's magazine called *Town*. They had bought a tailoring magazine *Man about Town* and broadened its appeal. Then with Nicholas Tomalin as editor and Tom Wolsey as art director, it became a lively and stylish magazine and a wonderful shop window for photographers and illustrators.

In the Sixties, Dennis Hackett edited a magazine called *Nova*, which was ahead of its time. I won't say that *Nova* invented adultery or orgasms, but it certainly helped to make these topics essential reading matter.

Dennis was always trying to find new ways to stretch people's talents. He (with Derek Birdsall as art director) was one of the first people to use my drawings to illustrate serious subjects.

He also packed me off to cover (in words and drawings) the newly opened Expo exhibition in Montreal, but when I returned with the story, Dennis had moved on to edit another magazine and my work went unused into my bottom drawer. That is the trouble with editors – by the time you get used to one, he has run off with another journal. Fickle chaps . . .

Town magazine: travel feature on Israel 1966.

Some of my best
friends are Jews,
but this is
ridiculous...

Calman in Israel

Israel is built on sand and paradoxes, and proud of both. They have developed the sand, created forests and cities; and they have nourished the paradoxes with the irrational eccentricities of every immigrant. Israel is really very small: the telephone directory for the whole country is the same size as the London A-D directory. Israel is new and tough. In many ways it is like an adolescent who has set up his own home – aggressive, proud and forever telling you what a great place he has. 'See that forest, I can remember when that was sand dunes...' I heard that so often that I thought it was the national anthem. So, forgive me, Israel but I haven't drawn a single forest. Trees are too difficult to draw anyway

Israel has one of the highest road-accident rates
in the world. Israelis blame the heat, the narrow roads
and other drivers.
Israel has welcomed Jews from all over the world.
Some have been accustomed to driving on the
left – others on the right.
A democratic compromise was called for, and all Israelis
drive down the middle of the road

Shalom! Shalom!

Everyone in Israel says 'shalom' when they meet...

The El Al hostesses are very attractive.
The one on my plane was very attentive
and I liked the way she fastened my
safety belt. We would have become better
friends if she hadn't told me that
she taught Judo in the Israeli Army. . .

Americans visiting the Hilton Shower at Tel Aviv..

eroot taxis are shared taxis and quite cheap. Seven passengers are carried and it's a tight fit. You get to
ow everyone else quite well – and if two of the other passengers are fat then you know them very well.
Sheroot can stop being a sheroot if the driver wishes to become an ordinary taxi. They don't have any
cial markings and you have to hail a taxi and ask: 'Are you a Sheroot?' which sounds very Surrealist.
e Sheroots are usually very old, battered American cars – Dodges, De Sotos, etc. . .

There is a living museum of very Orthodox Jews in Jerusalem.
It is a walled section of the city called Meir Sharim
and resembles a ghetto. The men wear the traditional
long silk coats, flat hats, long hair and beards.
This outfit makes a young man look like a very wise Rabbi.
They dislike being photographed and seem very shy.
People walked quickly by even at the sight of a sketchbook.
There is a large sign at the entrance asking women visitors to
dress modestly and not wear trousers

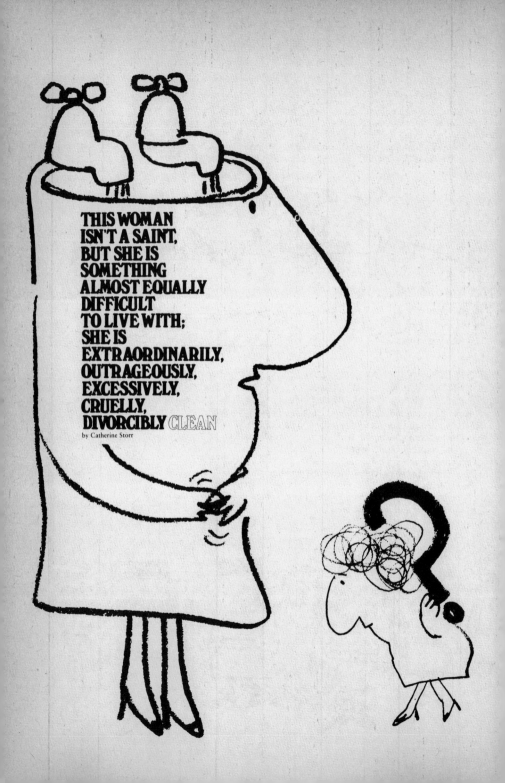

THIS WOMAN
ISN'T A SAINT,
BUT SHE IS
SOMETHING
ALMOST EQUALLY
DIFFICULT
TO LIVE WITH;
SHE IS
EXTRAORDINARILY,
OUTRAGEOUSLY,
EXCESSIVELY,
CRUELLY,
DIVORCIBLY CLEAN

by Catherine Storr

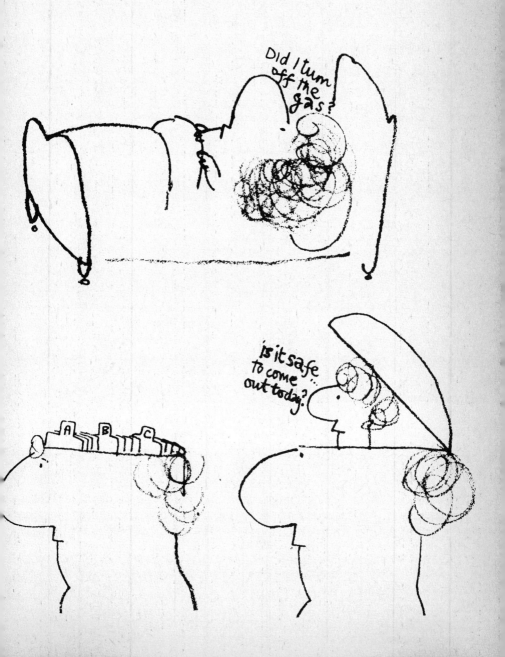

17.
A suitable case for framing...

In 1970 I was involved with the artist, Karen Usborne, who later became my second wife. She was rather a restless lady and she began to fret that she had no proper studio to work in. She was etching at that time and was tired of using the kitchen table. So was I – every time I wanted to make some toast, I had to clear away large sheets of copper and vats of black ink. The ink tended to get on my hands and the toast always tasted a bit funny after that.

So we looked for suitable spaces and the best one we found was an empty shop that had once sold knitting wool in Lambs Conduit Street. It was ideal: large and light with a self-contained room in the back. The rent was reasonable and the only drawback was that it was larger than even Karen (who liked large spaces) needed.

'Why don't we turn the front bit into an art gallery?' one of us said one day – just like Judy Garland used to say to Mickey Rooney, as in: 'Say – let's put on our own show in the Barn.'

And just like Mickey Rooney, I said, 'Great idea.' So I signed the lease, fitted the place up with lights, push-pin board and a desk and there we were. We had everything except any art to put on the walls.

We rang up friends and begged for anything they wanted to sell. Brian Robb (then Head of Illustration at the Royal College of Art) introduced us to some of his ex-students. Linda Kitson and Jim Haldane were the most interesting of these artists, and they fortunately had work to spare. Quentin Blake gave us some of his book illustrations. David Gentleman generously asked his wife, Sue, to print up some of his woodblocks especially for us. There were some bits and pieces of my own stuff that I consented to exhibit, and, of course, Karen's etchings, which had been rapidly proliferating in the kitchen.

There was not quite enough art, but carefully spread across the walls, it looked very nearly like an art gallery. In some ways, it looked more welcoming, because we decided to make the place look as casual and as inviting as possible. We called it 'The Workshop' to prevent customers from thinking we were too posh to enter. I did not want the gallery to look and feel like a bank vault, which some smart Mayfair galleries manage to do.

On the opening night, a power cut meant that people had to look at the pictures by candlelight. Very romantic but not very good for sales.

The next day we waited for the world to beat a path to our door. The first person who came in wanted to borrow two bob for a cup of coffee. The second showed us his wife's drawings of schooners.

'I was going to take them to Bond Street, but you're nearer,' he said.

The third looked like a customer, walked the entire length of the gallery, past all the drawings and prints and then asked, 'Do you still sell wool?'

I found that there were drawbacks to showing my own work.

One day a man came in and looked at my drawings and then snorted, 'Why does a scribble like that cost £10? A child could do better.'

'Yes,' I said, 'but it takes courage for an adult to draw as badly as that.'

On another day a couple came in and looked carefully at everything. The man picked up one of my books and compared the photograph on the back with my face.

At last he said, 'Are you Mr Calman?'

I blushed and modestly said, 'Yes'. I waited for the compliments to flow.

He turned to his wife, 'Darling, this is Mr Calman.' He paused and added, with great enthusiasm, 'You know, the one who draws those cartoons you don't understand.'

As time passed, we became very grateful for any customers – even ones who didn't understand my cartoons. We would sit for hours and not see another human being. The only sure way to attract customers was to shut for ten minutes and go for a cup of tea. There was a café next door, frequented mostly by taxi drivers, and it was a haven of company when the loneliness of the gallery became too acute. As soon as we went next door, customers would turn up and push outraged notes through the letter box – 'What kind of a gallery is this? You're NEVER here.'

I slowly learned how to organise exhibitions and keep the gallery alive. I realised that we could not simply open up every morning and hope for the best. We suddenly had rivals: Robin Ray and Bernard Levin opened a similar cartoon gallery in Gloucester Road, which flourished for a few years and then closed. Other galleries specialising in graphics and illustrations started up.

We were able to survive the lean months of the year because I had this other hobby – drawing cartoons. I was often amused by the casual way other people approached the craft of cartooning. One man came in and asked me if I could help him get started – he was out of work and needed some extra money.

'Could I do a bit part-time perhaps?' he asked.

'I don't know,' I replied. 'Would you try and do brain surgery part-time?'

I devised the annual Valentine Show to try and cheer up the overdraft during the bleak winter months; it became a popular show, giving young artists a chance to try out their skills without the strain of a one-man or woman show.

There were unexpected successes. We had a wall of Jim Haldane's work, which sat there for months, as he was completely unknown. Then a journalist saw them and wrote a piece about his work for *The Times*. She quoted Brian Robb as saying that he was probably the most exciting student to come out of the Royal College of Art since David Hockney. The day the article appeared, I was

startled suddenly to find the gallery full of customers. They had read the piece and had descended on us like locusts with wallets.

It was interesting to see the effect publicity had on people. It's as if reading about an artist gives people the confidence to buy his or her work – otherwise they feel too diffident to trust their own instincts.

Peter Brookes, Marie-Hélène Jeeves, Sara Midda, Posy, Paula Youens, Caroline Holden and Linda Kitson all had their first shows at the gallery. We inadvertently helped Linda Kitson to become the Official War Artist covering the Falklands conflict – though whether she should thank or blame me for that, I don't quite know. I believe that the relevant committee saw her exhibition of newspaper drawings at my gallery and was then convinced that she was the best person for the job.

Posy had two exhibitions that revealed a graphic and surreal side of her work that is not often seen in her black-and-white drawings. One was entirely about chocolates and the other about trains and their signals. We once even had the pleasure of seeing people queue up outside the gallery, waiting to come in and buy Sir Hugh Casson's watercolours.

There have also been some failures: one painter was very upset because people only wanted to buy the paintings he refused to sell. Another painter took all her work down the day after we had carefully put it up. She explained that she had to have it photographed for posterity. She did bring it back – the day before her show was scheduled to close.

Some work has been delightful to look at; some has made me dread going in to the gallery to see it.

One artist came in with ten huge and very ugly drawings on boards, at least ten feet tall. He asked my opinion of them.

'Not our cup of tea,' I said diplomatically.

'That's fine – no sweat,' he said, 'be back in ten minutes.' He disappeared, and returned two weeks later. I imagine he had needed a cheap place to store his work and kindly chose my gallery.

In 1979 Karen and I separated and then divorced. In 1984 I changed the name of the gallery to 'The Cartoon Gallery' – I felt like a change and the place was becoming

more like a cartoon emporium than anything else.

I have had to learn how to be an employer, which is a special skill, requiring all kinds of tact and delicacy. Some assistants have been delightful – some less so. One girl was well-meaning but rather depressed. She always wore her overcoat in the gallery, so that it looked as if she was about to leave. And she did.

Another young woman was frightfully nice and jolly but tended to arrive tired and emotional, full of tales of over-indulgence the night before. One girl left in the middle of the afternoon, pinning a note to the door: 'I can't stand it here any more.' She never returned, though she did send me a nice postcard from a Spanish resort, saying she was now happy and a single parent.

Another assistant became a good friend even though she read *The Daily Telegraph* and eventually married a Tory MP who moved to the right of Enoch Powell. No one's perfect.

Eventually, by chance, I found Pat Huntley, who now copes with all and sundry. She also kindly but firmly copes with me and my life. She appears to like people, a virtue not always as plentiful in art galleries as most customers would like. Pat dispenses so much tea and sympathy that I am thinking of re-naming the gallery, 'The Samovar'.

Over the years I have tried to show established artists as well as young, unknown ones. I organised the first exhibition in London, since his death, of Sir David Low's work. This was a great treat for me, as I think he is the finest political cartoonist Britain has produced this century – even if he was born in New Zealand.

We've also shown the cartoons of Paul Crum (who drew for *Night and Day* magazine before the war), Pont, Stampa, Frank Reynolds, Ronald Searle's lithographs and the genius of Heath Robinson.

I happened to meet Heath Robinson's widow and his daughter, Joan, through a chance conversation with a book editor, who knew them. I was invited to their home in Hornchurch, Essex, for afternoon tea.

Their house was exactly the kind of small suburban home that features in Heath Robinson's drawings. We had a delightful tea: thin sliced bread and butter, jam, fish-paste sandwiches, cake and a few memories of Heath Robinson. Mrs Robinson said that when they lived in

Highgate he worked in a little hut at the bottom of their garden.

'I could see him every day, pacing up and down – trying to think up ideas.'

After tea, she brought out several parcels wrapped up in old brown paper and tied carefully with string. Inside were all these wonderful Heath Robinson drawings, throbbing with life and humour. The contrast between the sparseness of the wrappings and the richness of the contents was oddly moving.

18. Two heads are better than one – even if it means halving the fee

I have sometimes wanted to collaborate with another designer, if only to break up the awful solitary quality of working alone. It is a great relief to have another person's opinion and ideas contributing to the solving of design problems. If designing is, as Sir Hugh Casson said somewhere, about making decisions, then it is easier to make them with another person around.

Philip Thompson and I have worked together for many years – and he has the scars to prove it. He has provided the skill to make this book the visual delight it undoubtedly is.

We met about twenty years ago, when we shared a small office in Tottenham Court Road, with another designer, Graham Bishop. The office was so small that if we all had to work there at the same time, one of us had to keep going outside to avoid severe claustrophobia.

Philip and I soon discovered that we shared several interests: old films, old jokes and a desire not to be bullied by Graham, who was a lovely man so long as you agreed with him. We used to share the office expenses (toilet rolls, Nescafé, tea bags, milk, etc.) and Graham would prepare detailed accounts, carefully splitting every purchase three ways. Discussing these bills seemed to take up a great deal of our time and energy.

Graham was an excellent designer and we had worked together on several books – he had designed *Bed-Sit* when it came out as a little book.

I decided that a change would be interesting, and asked Philip if he would work on one book jacket with me for Penguin Books. We completed the job and found that we had enjoyed the experience – in a mild sort of way. Philip's great virtue, to my mind, is that he knows when to leave well alone. He dislikes cluttering up a design with irrelevant detail, and so do I.

Over the years, we have worked on many books and have never disagreed about how to solve the problems

He has to be NICE about Philip or else this book will never reach the PRINTERS..

involved. We have even been able to discuss a design over the telephone – visualising what each other is describing.

Philip has also designed most of the gallery invitations over the past fifteen years, giving them a much-needed sense of humour and invention.

Pelican Library of Business and Management

Once in Golconda
A True Drama of Wall Street 1920-38
John Brooks

Pelican Original

Taxation Polic
Edited by Bernard Crick and
William A. Robson

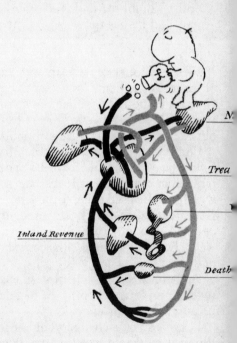

N.

Trea

Inland Revenue

Death

Penguin book jackets designed with Philip Thompson

a Pelican Original

Noise

Rupert Taylor

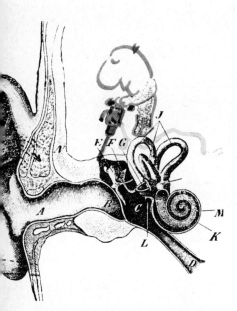

Pelican Library of Business and Management

Business Adventures

John Brooks

'My God' began as a single joke that popped into my head one day. I was doodling a series of God figures sitting on clouds when I thought of Him saying to himself, 'That's one whole day gone and all I've done is turn the light on.' I couldn't think of any other jokes about Him, so I put that idea aside. I didn't throw it away since I always hope that ideas will fester and improve in the dark of the desk drawer.

About a year later, when I was looking for something else, I came across this scribble and wondered again what God thought about when He was sitting up there on His cloud. There is a strong Jewish comic tradition of people talking to God directly and my mother was fond of quoting these conversations from Jewish folklore. I imagine that my own cartoon speculations originate from memories of these stories. And of course I often speak to a 'God' inside my head when I am at the end of my tether – where I often end up when trying to make jokes.

When I had drawn about half a dozen jokes I liked I showed them to Hunter Davies, who was then editing the 'Look' pages of *The Sunday Times*. He ran them in the paper and they became a regular feature. The great bonus of regular features is that their deadlines force you to find new material; there is something deeply stirring about the approach of a deadline. The challenge of a blank page (a hole that must be filled) usually produces the adrenalin that in turn triggers off ideas. Too much adrenalin can induce panic, of course . . . and then – God help you.

In more recent years I have sat at my desk at *The Times*, staring miserably at the blank white paper and wanted to scream. I scribble, I doodle, I write odd words down on bits of paper, I make lists of associated words and images – anything to stir up the pot and produce something nourishing. I know that if I once walked out without doing a cartoon I would be like a trapeze artist who had fallen and then lost his nerve forever.

A few weeks after 'My God' started in *The Sunday Times*, I got a phone call from Ernest Hecht (of Souvenir Press) asking me if I'd thought of making a book out of them. I said I liked the idea but felt obliged to offer the idea first to Tom Maschler (of Jonathan Cape) who had published my last three cartoon books.

I made an appointment to see Tom to discuss this and

Thou Shalt
Not break
thine
appointments.

the next week took my cartoons along to the Cape offices in Bedford Square. I announced myself and sat in the waiting room. A secretary came to apologise and said that Tom would see me soon. I waited for nearly an hour and at last was admitted into Tom's magnificent period office.

He was sitting at his large desk, surrounded by piles of manuscripts. There were additional piles on the floor at his feet. He sighed and gestured towards them.

'I'm sorry to have kept you waiting,' he said, 'but you can see how it is. It's hopeless trying to talk to you properly today. Could we possibly make it next week? Do you mind?'

What could I say? 'If you were too busy why – in God's name – did you keep me waiting downstairs all this time, you CREEP you? Why be so bloody, just because you are a publisher and I'm only a humble cartoonist? I'd love to cut off your head, stew it and then stick it on the railings of Bedford Square.' Instead I said, 'Oh sure . . . of course .'

Tom smiled in what he thought was a charming manner and we said goodbye.

I went home and wished I had a cat to kick. The next day I rang Ernest Hecht and offered him the God book.

I liked Ernest – for one thing, he always kept his appointments. He was enthusiastic, energetic and slightly eccentric. He was happy to talk about my book but also happy to move on to more important matters like football and ice-cream. Ernest knew where the best ice-cream in the world could be purchased. He once boasted to me that he had eaten three enormous Knickerbocker Glories, one after the other, at the Champs Elysées Drugstore in Paris. I always treated him with great respect after that.

My God was published in 1970 and made very little impact on the world. A few clergymen wrote to me, either loving it or loathing it and saying it was sacrilegious. One American cleric wrote from a town called Mystic, telling me that he had organised a study group to meet and find the textual references in the Bible that matched my cartoons. Another parson told me that he used the jokes to lighten his sermons. I hope this will stand me in good stead on the Day of Judgement.

20. Go west young man

One day I unexpectedly received a letter from an American agent called Toni Mendez. She had seen some of my work when visiting Ernest Hecht and had liked it. The letter was extremely flattering and suggested that I was exactly the kind of genius the American markets needed. She thought that she could get my work syndicated in the United States.

I should explain that syndication means having the same drawing bought and reproduced by lots and lots of newspapers, so that you earn more money for the same sweat. It is every cartoonist's dream – if you can find some magic formula that works, like Garfield the Cat.

I discounted most of Toni's letter as American gush, but sent her some samples of my work. She replied, amazingly quickly by British standards, that the Field Newspaper Syndicate (who syndicated many famous strips, including Andy Capp) wanted me to try a daily comic strip for them. I knew this was beyond my powers of invention but offered her an idea for a single panel about men and women. Field liked the idea and suggested a brilliant title: 'Men and Women'.

The editor, Dick Sherry, came to London on business and invited me to breakfast with him at his hotel. This was indeed the Big Time: American-style business breakfasts. Dick turned out to be a very nice, soft-spoken man with a wry sense of humour, and not the aggressive hustler I expected. We discussed everything – the contract, the kind of jokes I might do, other cartoonists, and why his hotel always ran out of croissants as soon as he came down to breakfast.

'Why don't they just bake more?' he asked plaintively.

'Ah – you don't understand the English,' I said, 'they like shortages. That's why the War was so popular.'

In due course a very long, complicated contract arrived – over 20 pages. I agreed to supply Field with six cartoons a week for a trial run of five years, to be renewed for another five years, if all went well. I was excited and terrified. It felt like being something very close to a professional – and the thought kept me awake at nights. I preferred to think of myself as a gifted amateur – a man who somehow managed to get his work printed, in spite of his failings.

To some extent I still like the idea of amateurism – and usually keep my desk in a perpetual state of unreadiness: blunt pencils, no proper set square and a rubber that keeps vanishing when I need it.

Dick suggested I do at least two months' cartoons in advance, to get ahead. 'You'll be glad you did', he said – and he was right. The contracts were signed and I was off. It became a peculiar ritual in my life. Every week I posted six cartoons off to America and was greeted by a deafening silence. At first I got enthusiastic letters from Dick, telling me how sales were going, but after a while, the only feedback I had were editorial comments and spelling corrections. (Americans do not spell properly: Theater, color, honor, etc.). I discovered that the syndicate was very careful not to offend its readers – most of whom lived in Middle America. One cartoon captioned 'Flying is hell on the feet' was returned to me, as 'hell' was considered too strong for American tastes.

I supplied America with jokes for over five years and then decided I had to stop. I was beginning to dread the weekly approach of my deadline. If I wanted to take a week off I had to supply an extra week's cartoons. I had cannibalised every scrap of an idea from my filing cabinet and my extensive researches into marital strife were wearing me out.

I had enjoyed a great deal of the experience – especially the sense of working for this enormous country. I had even braved the Newspaper Cartoonists' Annual Dinners at the Plaza Hotel in New York, where I listened to Oscar-style speeches by cartoonists thanking their mothers for lending them their pencils and making their success possible.

The irony of this episode is that most of these drawings, originally drawn for American consumption, have been edited into collections published here in Great Britain with reasonable success by Methuen (still available – advertisement) but that no American publisher has ever risked publishing them.

I have had some delightful lunches with editors in New York – usually with Toni Mendez present as marriage broker – and they have laughed and enthused about my work. 'We all love it, Mel,' they cry – and then comes the long silence followed by the letter of regret: 'The Sales Department feels that your work, wonderful though it is . . . etc . . . etc.'

Ah, well . . .

Men and Women: cartoon feature for Field Newspaper Syndicate

Men and Women: cartoon feature for Field Newspaper Syndicate

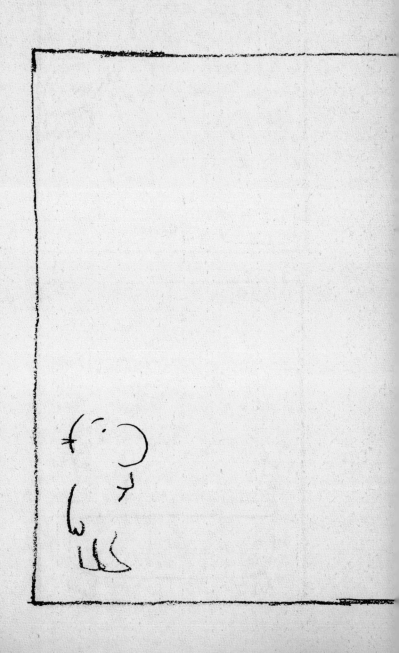

And now, the moment you have been waiting for – a few words about white space. I have always had constant battles with newspaper sub-editors for space. White paper is considered a terrible waste of good paper; they want every inch filled with words.

you call it 'SPACE'
but I call it
TRYING to get away
from ME..

I like a certain amount of air around my drawings and I usually have to fight for this. If a sub-editor sees two blank inches above my little man, he itches to chop this off and fill it with a news item. I have sometimes had to add a superfluous lampshade hanging from the top of the drawing, merely to defend this territory.

I once had to stand-in for Jak on the *Evening Standard*. I drew my cartoon with a little man looking lost and wistful in the middle of the vast Jak-sized space. It looked rather dramatic, I thought, but the editor urgently requested me to add some furniture to help fill up the area.

The trouble is, I think, that almost all editors are word-orientated. They usually have been educated in the Oxbridge tradition and have very little understanding of visual matters. They might enjoy looking at the odd oil painting in their spare time, but the world of graphic design is a closed book to them.

A newspaper is basically a lot of voices screaming for attention: advertisements, photos, news, features and more ads. A cartoon has only a very small space to compete with all this and I think that every square inch is needed to help focus attention on the drawing. I take a great deal of trouble in placing the figures inside the cartoon area – it may look as if it has all been thrown together by chance, but that is not so. And so I am very jealous of my patch.

Nonsense – The TIMES is always RIGHT..

There was one editor, I remember, who seemed to have only one graphic requirement of my work, and that was that the eye of the reader had to be led into the page. (He must have read this dictum somewhere in a book about design.) This meant that he wanted the people in my cartoons to walk into the page – i.e. from left to right. If I forgot this golden rule he would gently but firmly ask me to redraw it. Needless to say, he rarely commented on the joke itself.

In fact, the business of persuading newspaper people to laugh at one's jokes is a difficult and painful affair. Editors are a tough breed and don't like to have their rugged features broken up by laughter creases. Their usual reaction to a cartoon is to ask how deep it is, so that they can mark the measurement on their layouts. If I ever slip under their guard and evoke a small smile, I consider myself extremely happy and go home dancing on a cloud of pure euphoria.

BOMBS FOUND ON PLANE!
TALKS FAIL
HOSTAGES KILLED
CRISIS: REACTOR LEAKS
JOBLESS UP!
IRISH TALKS: LITTLE HOPE
What's the problem?

I have come to rely on the judgement of the picture desk at *The Times*. There are the men who mark-up the drawings and pictures before they disappear into the process department. If one of these men laughs, then I know I have scored a bull's-eye.

I recall meeting a sub-editor in Fleet Street years after I had been working with him on the *Daily Express*. He had been looking at my drawings for over five years – accepting them and using them in his layouts. We stopped and looked at each other.

'How are you?' I said.

'Fine', he said. 'I'm sorry – but I can't remember where we met before. Was it at some party, perhaps?'

I knew then that I had done the right thing by leaving the *Express* when I did.

22. Six days make one weak

Most of my career has been chance. I came to draw for *The Times* because of a chance encounter. *The Times* was closed in 1978–79 during the Thomson period of ownership and when it was about to return, I was asked by the promotion department to give them a suitable cartoon to celebrate the event. I sent them a cartoon showing a couple at the breakfast table, with the man reading *The Times* and the wife saying, 'I suppose that's the end of conversation.'

By some fluke, this cartoon was seen by the editor, William Rees-Mogg, who wanted to use it on the front page on the day *The Times* returned. They did, and I thought no more about it.

The next day I was invited to go and have lunch with Louis Heren, the deputy editor. We went to Simpson's in the Strand and I was very excited as this was the only time I have ever been taken to lunch by a Fleet Street editor. (I discount the time the editor of the *Sunday Telegraph* took me and Stanley Price to a cafeteria in Fleet Street, where we queued up with our trays and had to take our time finding our wallets, in case we found them before he found his.)

Louis Heren said that Rees-Mogg had liked the look of the cartoon on the front page, and would I like to try doing one every day? I was already drawing for *The Sunday Times*, so said I ought to ask Harry Evans. Although both papers were then owned by Lord Thomson, they tried to be as separate as possible. *The Times* considered *The Sunday Times* rather brash, and *The Sunday Times* thought *The Times* snobbish.

Harry was not exactly enthusiastic about the idea but said he wouldn't stand in my way; so we compromised by my agreeing to draw for *The Times* on Monday till Friday – leaving a gap on Saturday to clear the public palate for the glories of Sunday.

My first day was tense; I felt as if I had never drawn for newspapers before. The atmosphere was formal after *The*

Sunday Times. I went to the afternoon conference and found everyone sitting in a semi-circle around William Rees-Mogg, who was sitting in a cane rocking chair, sipping china tea, and looking like the headmaster of a decent public school.

He did not use people's names, simply calling on them by departments: Home, Foreign, Sport, Features, Letters and so on. I half expected him to call me 'Humour', but he never felt the need to ask for my contributions.

I showed my cartoon ideas to Louis, who was amiable, if a little over-concerned not to offend the readers. The Royal Family and the Catholic Church were considered especially sacred subjects.

I soon settled into a routine of going into the paper in the late afternoons and talking to the night editor about possible subjects. I watched the six o'clock news on telly and scanned the *Standard* for other late news – and to see what Heath's cartoon was about. There is always the danger of making the same joke as another cartoonist.

Over the years I think I have learned how to avoid making jokes in bad taste. I try not to be too bland but I

also feel that I am a guest at someone's breakfast table and if they are offended, they might not ask me in next time.

The most difficult areas are news items about sieges and wars, when people are likely to be killed, and jokes seem extremely tasteless. During the Falklands conflict, I often wanted to make some pointed comment but was restrained by realising that some readers' relatives were risking and losing their lives.

I did try to publish a cartoon with two penguins on a rock, the one saying to the other, 'If I get killed, I want a British funeral', which seemed to me to be a fair comment on the awful tragedy of the war, but the editor did not approve and the cartoon was spiked.

I did several cartoons about the Falklands which were used, however. One was printed fairly early on in the conflict: a man sitting on a rock saying, 'This is another fine mess someone's gotten me into'.

I was pleased to receive a letter from the Officer Commanding the Royal Marines Company, who had been involved in re-taking the Survey Base at South Georgia on 25 April 1982.

We left England secretly on 9 April 1982 knowing that we were to move ahead of the main force to carry out this task. Before departing I was amused by your cartoon . . . . My company is now established as garrison here for the near future and your drawing seems to us particularly apt for our situation. First, would you give me permission for us to use exclusively your drawing on a T-shirt which will be produced for members of the South Georgia Operation only? Secondly, would you allow me to hold the original?

I wrote to him, giving permission and sending the original. In July I got a second letter from him, thanking me for the original. The letter went on:

It may amuse you to know that your letter replying to my request went all the way to South Georgia and finally arrived on my desk (in England) two days ago, 16,000 miles on a ½p stamp.

I regret the campaign has sad memories for our family as my brother, Richard, another Royal, was shot down and killed in his helicopter at Goose Green. However, there is always time for humour even in such times.

I found that comment very moving and it made me feel slightly less hopeless about doing my job every day.

Disasters and wars are extremely difficult subjects to comment on. They cannot be ignored and yet they must be treated with great delicacy. A smart wisecrack can look very silly the next morning, alongside the news that people have been killed overnight. (For that reason I usually avoid all sieges until the hostages are safe and sound.)

I sometimes do find an appropriate comment. After the Munich massacre during the Olympic Games, I attempted a pictorial comment, adding a bomb to one of the Olympic circles.

Pictorial, rather than verbal comments, are often very effective ways of solving this ever-present problem of taste.

Another problem is trying to be funny about on-going situations that will not go away. The miners' strike was one; unemployment is another. It is difficult to make jokes about other people's suffering – and yet, if one is too sentimental, the joke lacks the bite that makes it memorable.

INSIGHT on
The Munich Massacre
Four-page special, pp 15-18

There are especial difficulties for a topical cartoonist who cannot draw likenesses of political figures. I have had to use all my ingenuity to overcome this defect. For example, since I cannot draw Mrs Thatcher I have to resort to drawing the front door of No 10 Downing Street, in order to show that the voice talking is hers. I have had to draw the Queen from the back – not her best feature, perhaps.

I wanted to show Mrs Reagan and Mrs Gorbachov talking together during the Geneva Summit, as I imagined them gossiping about their respective husbands, and had to draw their hands instead of their faces. *(See page 108.)*

I enjoy limitations as they stimulate my inventiveness. In fact, the whole situation of drawing inside a small space like a pocket cartoon (a single column of 65 mm) presents many interesting problems.

There is the severe danger of visual monotony. There is barely room in the space for two figures or one figure and some prop. Usually the cartoon has to contain some reference to the story in the form of a newspaper headline or placard, since the cartoon must be self-contained. A reader rarely has the time or patience, I feel, to puzzle about what the joke refers to.

I know that all my drawings look alike – some of my best friends keep telling me this. But the truth is not quite so simple. I do try to achieve some variations – even if they are minor – in the format. I try to vary the scale of the figures, or the way they are placed inside the cartoon box. I also use the words themselves to make the drawing graphically more interesting. I realised a long time ago that, since all the type in a newspaper is horizontal, a caption needs to be written at an angle if it is going to be noticed and not vanish into the general scrum of type clamouring for attention.

I also prefer the hand-written caption instead of the type-set one, to provide further variety. I can give emphasis to certain words by making them **bolder**. I also try to break up the lines to give the impression of speaking. I try to listen to the words inside my head and write them to sound as crisp and succinct as possible. I spend a lot of time re-writing these captions to achieve a natural rhythm.

23. *The Times* – they are a'changing

There have been many changes since I started drawing for a living thirty years ago. The world is slightly crazier – more people seem to want to blow other people up. Newspapers have changed and are still changing. *The Times* has moved to Wapping, where electricians have become printers and typewriters have become extinct.

I still have the illusion that I might grow up and have a real job one day, instead of messing about with pencils and bits of paper.

In the meantime, I just go on trying to avoid cholesterol and help people to cope with living under a Tory government.

If I'd known I was going to WRITE my memoirs, I'd have lived a MORE interesting LIFE ...